The SIMD Model of Parallel Computation

Robert Cypher   Jorge L.C. Sanz

The SIMD Model of Parallel Computation

With 13 Illustrations

Springer-Verlag

New York Berlin Heidelberg London Paris
Tokyo Hong Kong Barcelona Budapest

Robert Cypher
IBM T. J. Watson
   Research Center
Yorktown Heights, NY 10598,
   USA

Jorge L. C. Sanz
University of Illinois at
   Urbana-Champaign
Department of Electrical
   and Computer Engineering
Urbana, IL 61801, USA

Cover illustration: Mesh connected computer. Detail from Fig. 4.1, p. 21

Library of Congress Cataloging-in-Publication Data
Cypher, Robert.
    The SIMD model of parallel computation / Robert Cypher, Jorge L. C.
Sanz.
      p.   cm.
    Includes bibliographical references and index.
    ISBN 0-387-94139-8
    1. Parallel processing (Electronic computers)   2. Computer
architecture.   I. Sanz, J. L. C. (Jorge L. C.), 1955–   ,
II. Title.
QA76.58.C96   1994
004′.35—dc20   93-27497

Printed on acid-free paper.

Production managed by Terry Kornak; manufacturing supervised by Vincent Scelta.
Typeset by Asco Trade Typesetting Ltd., Hong Kong.
Printed and bound by R. R. Donnelley & Sons, Inc., Harrisonburg, VA.
Printed in the United States of America.

9 8 7 6 5 4 3 2 1

ISBN 0-387-94139-8 Springer-Verlag New York Berlin Heidelberg
ISBN 3-540-94139-8 Springer-Verlag Berlin Heidelberg New York

Contents

CHAPTER 1

Introduction

1.1 Background

There are many paradigmatic statements in the literature claiming that this is the decade of parallel computation. A great deal of research is being devoted to developing architectures and algorithms for parallel machines with thousands, or even millions, of processors. Such massively parallel computers have been made feasible by advances in VLSI (very large scale integration) technology. In fact, a number of computers having over one thousand processors are commercially available. Furthermore, it is reasonable to expect that as VLSI technology continues to improve, massively parallel computers will become increasingly affordable and common.

However, despite the significant progress made in the field, many fundamental issues still remain unresolved. One of the most significant of these is the issue of a general purpose parallel architecture. There is currently a huge variety of parallel architectures that are either being built or proposed. The problem is whether a single parallel computer can perform *efficiently* on *all* computing applications.

When considering this question, it is important to notice that there is no unique serial architecture that dominates over all of the others. The advent of special purpose workstations and dedicated architectures has provided cost-effective solutions to many demanding computational problems. Today, nobody would perform low-level image processing without a pipeline of dedicated components performing specific image functions.[207] Signal processing chip sets and systolic arrays [140] are well-suited to many numerically intensive problems. Graphics stations are exclusively dedicated to certain design problems, and in many cases, these computers are single-user oriented. In a completely analogous manner, vector computers have been heavily used by the numerical computing community. These devices are specialized attachments to central processors. It is unlikely that people will stop using them in favor of large-scale, general purpose serial computers. Thus, the profusion of parallel architectures is not very different from the situation with regard to serial architectures.

To understand the arguments for and against a single, general purpose parallel architecture, it is important to recognize the motivation for parallel processing. Parallelism may be regarded as a vehicle to accomplish two different goals. First, it may become a viable way to provide a given amount of computation at a lower cost. Second, it may be used to extend the range of problems that can be solved by computers, regardless of the cost. Of course, these two motivations may coexist, and indeed, they are the ultimate goal of many of today's research projects. Research on general purpose parallel computers could be beneficial for future systems that will provide inexpensive computer power. These computers will be aimed at supporting a very large number of simultaneous users, much in the same way as today's powerful mainframes. Software will provide users with multiprogramming environments, time-sharing operating systems, and programming languages oriented to a rich variety of applications.

On the other hand, it is unlikely that these systems will be able to provide the amount of computing power that is demanded by applications involving numerical analysis, computer vision systems, or physics simulations. Furthermore, the environment provided by a general purpose system is not the most appropriate one for the computing needs of these users. There will be other, more specialized, parallel computers operating as backend coprocessors to satisfy the computing needs of those sophisticated users. These computers will be tailored to classes of applications and will play a role similar to today's special purpose attachments, such as vector processors. The software and hardware involved in these computers will be different from those required by general purpose parallel systems. Time and cost overheads introduced by some software and hardware features are considerable and can be justified only in the presence of a general computing environment. An insightful discussion on this topic, titled "shared memory and the corollary of modest potential", is given by L. Snyder.[230]

Overall, the parallel processing field should not be polarized. It is unlikely that a single parallel computer or architecture will satisfy the computing requirements of all possible applications. In retrospect, the short, but rich, history of computing demonstrates that there is a diversity of serial machines tailored to different applications. There is, and probably will continue to be, a large zoo of parallel computers. Ultimately, the nature of the application areas and cost considerations will make some of them more useful or appealing than others. On the other hand, it is likely that some consolidation will occur as parallel architectures become better understood and more widely used. The need for consolidation is particularly acute in the area of models for parallel programming. If a small number of models of parallel computation can be agreed upon, programmers and algorithm designers can focus on these models and create applications that will be portable across a variety of parallel architectures.

In this monograph, a tour through this zoo of parallel architectures is presented. For each architecture that is studied, algorithms that are tailored to the given architecture will be presented. Although a range of applications areas will be considered, a set of basic operations related to image processing, sorting and routing, and numerical computing will be examined for each of the architectures. These algorithms will be useful in their own right, but will also serve as a means of comparing the different types of parallel computers and will aid in selecting the correct architecture for a given problem area. The emphasis will be on the SIMD (single instruction-stream, multiple data-stream) model of parallel computation and its implementation on both SIMD and MIMD (muliple instruction-stream, multiple data-stream) architectures.[85,231]

1.2 Notation

N is used to represent the size of the input to a problem, such as the number of pixels in an image to be processed or the number of entries in each of two matrices to be multiplied. P is used to represent the number of processors in a parallel machine. A function $F(X)$ is said to be $O(G(X))$ if, for all sufficiently large X, there exists a constant C, such that $F(X) \le C * G(X)$.

If X is a nonnegative integer, then the Y-bit representation of X will be written as $(X_{(Y-1)}, X_{(Y-2)}, \ldots, X_{(0)})$, and the i-th bit of X will be denoted by $X_{(i)}$ (where the 0-th bit is the least significant bit). Also, $X^{(i)}$ is the integer obtained by complementing the i-th bit of X.

The notation $\log X$ will denote the base-2 logarithm of X. The function $\log^{(0)} X = X$, and for all integers $i > 0$, $\log^{(i)} X = \log(\log^{(i-1)} X)$. The function $\log^* X$ equals the smallest nonnegative integer i, such that $\log^{(i)} X \le 1$.

1.3 Outline

The remaining chapters are organized as follows. Chapters 2 and 3 present an overview of parallel architectures and programming methodologies, respectively. Chapters 4 through 12 provide a critical survey of various parallel architectures and algorithms, based on the topology of the connections between the processors. Specifically, Chapters 4 and 5 look at mesh connected computers, Chapters 6 and 7 focus on pyramid computers, and Chapters 8 through 11 are devoted to hypercube and related computers. For each topology, several existing and proposed parallel machines are discussed and compared. Also, an analysis of parallel algorithms for image processing and scientific and symbolic tasks is presented. The effects of architectural decisions on algorithm design are examined in detail. Finally, some conclusions are outlined in Chapter 12.

CHAPTER 2

Parallel Computer Architectures

The basic types of parallel computer architectures are examined in this chapter. The focus here will be on the physical design of the computer. In Chapter 3, the different high-level models that can be presented to a programmer of a parallel machine will be studied.

2.1 Memory Organization

The physical location of the memory in a parallel computer can be classified as being either *shared* or *distributed*. In a shared (also called "centralized") memory parallel architecture, there is a set of memory locations that are not local to any processor. In order for the processors to access these shared memory locations, they must issue read or write requests that are routed to the memory via a bus or a switching network. In addition to these shared memory locations, each processor in a shared memory architecture has a local private memory in which it can store private data, copies of shared data, and pointers to the shared memory.

In a distributed memory parallel computer, each memory location is local to some processor. A processor can access its own local memory directly. However, to access another processor's local memory, it must send a message to the processor that owns the memory. A processor and its local memory will sometimes be referred to as a *processing element* (PE).

2.2 Communication Medium

In both shared memory and distributed memory computers, a processor must communicate in order to access data that are not stored in its local memory. In shared memory computers, this communication occurs between processors and the shared memory, while in distributed memory computers, it occurs between pairs of processors. There are three techniques that are used for performing this communication, namely, busses, switching networks, and direct processor-to-processor links. Computers that use these communication techniques are called *bus-based*, *switch-based*, and *processor-based*, respectively. These distinctions are not always sharp, since a single computer can have multiple communication media. For example, some computers have both busses and direct links between pairs of processors.

Both switch-based and processor-based architectures can use either *packet routing* or *circuit switching* to deliver messages. In packet routing, messages are divided into packets that are routed to their destinations. Packets compete with other packets for resources (such as wires and buffers) in a dynamic manner. In circuit switching, an entire path between the message sender and receiver is established. All of the communication links along this path are reserved for the given sender-receiver pair. They cannot be accessed by other senders. Once the path is established, the sender may transmit messages without fear of interference.

There are also several switching modes for packet routing. In store-and-forward routing, the packet "hops" between buffers, and the head of the packet waits until the tail of the packet has been stored in the buffer. In *wormhole routing*[63] and *virtual cut-through routing*,[129] each packet is divided into small units called *flits*. The flits follow one another in a snakelike manner from the sender to the receiver. Thus, if a packet consists of only one flit, these techniques store the entire packet after each hop, and a store-and-forward implementation is obtained. On the other hand, if a message contains a very large number of flits, the first flits will arrive at the receiver before the later flits have even been sent. As a result, the entire path between the sender and receiver will be occupied, as is the case with circuit switching. Wormhole and virtual cut-through routing behave differently when a packet encounters congestion. In wormhole routing, the entire packet is stopped in place, thus, blocking all of the communication links that it occupies. In virtual cut-through routing, the tail of the packet continues to advance, and the entire packet is stored in the node where the congestion was encountered.

In a processor-based distributed memory computer, only certain pairs of processors are connected by direct communication links. Thus, access to another processor's memory may require that a message be routed to the other processor via several intermediate processors. Some processor-based computers allow data to be transferred in both directions simultaneously along a single communication link, while others require that data be transferred in one direction at a time. Some processor-based machines, called *strong communication* machines, allow a single processor to send a different data item over each of its communication links simultaneously. Other processor-based machines, called *weak communication* machines, limit each processor to sending a single data item over a single communication link at a time.

2.3 Topology

Whether busses, switches, or direct links between processors are used for the communication, the communication network can have a wide range of topologies. In bus-based systems, a single bus or multiple busses may be used. When multiple busses are present, every bus may be connected to every processor and/or memory bank, or different busses may be connected to different subsets of processors and memory banks.

One of the most common topologies for switch-based computers is the Omega network.[145] An Omega network connects N inputs to N outputs by means of $\log N$ stages of switches. Each stage consists of $N/2$ switches, each of which has two inputs and two outputs. An Omega network can perform many useful permutations of the inputs to the outputs, but it cannot perform every permutation. As a result, it is possible that some collisions will occur within the network, even though each input is accessing a different output.

Another switching network topology that has been used in a parallel computer is the Benes network.[19,20] Benes networks can be defined for various switch sizes. When it is composed of switches with two inputs and two outputs, the Benes network has $2(\log N) - 1$ stages, each of which consists of $N/2$ switches. A Benes network is capable of performing every permutation of the inputs to the outputs. However, it is time-consuming to calculate how the switches should be set in order to implement a given permutation without having collisions. Therefore, the Benes network is typically used only if the patterns of communication are known in advance and the switch settings can be calculated by the compiler.

A rich class of topologies has been proposed for processor-based parallel computers. These include trees, two- and three-dimensional meshes, pyramids, hypercubes, shuffle-exchanges, and cube-connected cycles. Processor-based architectures will be emphasized in this monograph, and the topologies for these architectures will be studied in depth in the remaining chapters.

2.4 Control

An important characteristic of a parallel machine is whether it operates in an SIMD or an MIMD mode. In an MIMD architecture, different processors can perform different operations at a single time. As a result, each processor in an MIMD machine must have its own copy of its program as well as instruction fetching and decoding logic in order to interpret its program.

In an SIMD architecture, all of the processors are forced to execute the same instruction at the same time. Thus, in an SIMD machine, it is possible to have only one copy of the program and a single controller that fetches the instructions, decodes them, and broadcasts the control signals to all of the processors. However, most SIMD machines offer some degree of processor autonomy by allowing a subset of the processors to ignore the current instruction while the remaining processors execute it. This is accomplished by placing a binary register, called a *mask register*, in each processor and designating certain instructions as being *maskable*. When a maskable instruction is executed, those processors that have a 1 in their mask register perform the instruction, while those processors that have a 0 in their mask register are idle.

Most SIMD architectures do not have a direct data connection from the controller to the processors. However, there are situations in which the controller must broadcast a data value to all of the processors. This can be accomplished by having the processors calculate the number one bit at a time. For instance, if each processor has the ability to calculate arbitrary boolean functions, then they can be directed to calculate the function that always returns TRUE for those bit positions of the broadcast value that contain a 1 and to calculate the function that always returns FALSE for the remaining bit positions.

In addition to distinguishing between SIMD and MIMD control, there are two other ways in which the type of control may be classified. First, in a distributed memory machine, the local memory addresses of the operands and results can be the same for every processor at a given time or they can be different in separate processors. The former case will be referred to as *uniform addressing*, while the latter will be referred to as *independent addressing*. It is possible to have independent addressing even when all of the processors are operating under the direction of a single controller; this can be accomplished by using indirection.

Second, processor-based distributed memory computers with weak communication can be separated into two categories. Assume that the communication links leaving each processor are numbered. If every processor must send data along the same communication link (such as the third one) at a given time, the machine will be said to operate with *uniform communication*. If, instead, separate processors can send messages along different communication links at a given time, the machine will be said to operate with *independent communication*. Independent communication can be implemented when there is a single controller by using indirection to choose the communication port from which data will be sent.

2.5 Clocking

Parallel computers use several different clocking schemes. One option is the use of a single global clock that is broadcast to all of the processors. This option is particularly natural for SIMD machines, but it can be used in MIMD machines as well. A difficulty with using only a single clock is that the clock signal may reach different processors at different times. This phenomenon is called *clock skew*. Clock skew puts a limit on the cycle time of the clock, because the skew between any two communicating processors must be kept below the cycle time to guarantee that the processors are operating on the same cycle. Fortunately, it appears that clock skew can be effectively controlled by careful design of the clock lines. For example, clock skew in the 4096 processor J-machine is kept below 2 ns.[175]

Another clocking scheme is the use of a separate clock for each processor. This avoids the problem of clock skew, but it creates problems associated with communicating between separate clocked regions. When two clocked regions exchange data, arbitration between the clocks is required. The time required by this arbitration depends on the relative phases of the clocks, but it can be significant. If the architecture is processor-based, then each communication between connected processors requires a separate clock arbitration. If the architecture is switch-based, then the switching network can be asynchronous. In this case, both clock skew and clock arbitration problems are minimized. Furthermore, an asynchronous network has the potential to run more quickly than a synchronous one. This is because in an asynchronous network, data are passed on as soon as they are ready, while in a synchronous network, the cycle time is set to the time required by the slowest operation. However, asynchronous networks often require some overhead, both in terms of wires and time, to perform handshaking.

Yet another clocking scheme is possible when the routing is circuit-switched. In this scheme, each communication link consists of data wires and a strobe wire. Once a path has been established between a source and destination node, successive data and strobe wires along the path are electrically connected to one another, forming parallel data and strobe paths. Then, data are placed on the data path, and the strobe path is used to clock the associated data. Specifically, each transition on the strobe path indicates that new data are present on the data path. In this scheme, each communication path operates synchronously, although separate data paths have separate clocks. The advantage of this technique is that it avoids the handshaking required by asynchronous techniques and the clock arbitration delays required by other synchronous techniques. The disadvantages are the need for extra wires (for the strobe signal and for status information that is sent from the destination processor to the source processor) and the requirement that circuit switching be used. This type of clocking scheme is used in the Intel iPSC/2 computer.[178]

2.6 Processor Design

Although it would be desirable to use powerful processors, cost and technological considerations force a tradeoff between the number of processors and processor power. Commercial machines with 1K or more 32-bit processors are available, where each processor occupies a single chip or board. These processors could be either general purpose reduced instruction set (RISC) processors or custom processors that have been optimized for parallel processing.[115,173] As the number of processors increases into the tens of thousands, multiple processors are placed on a single chip and the word size of the processors decreases. MasPar has recently introduced a machine with up to 16K processors, each of which operates on 4-bit quantities.[159]

Other massively parallel machines have used bit-serial (1-bit word size) processors.[17,106,172] A bit-serial processor can typically perform an arbitrary boolean function of two 1-bit inputs. Also, bit-serial processors usually have the power of a full adder, which is a unit that takes three 1-bit operands, $A1$, $A2$, and $A3$, and provides two 1-bit outputs, S and C, where $S = A1$ XOR $A2$ XOR $A3$ and $C = (A1$ AND $A2)$ OR $(A1$ AND $A3)$ OR $(A2$ AND $A3)$. That is, S is the sum bit and C is the carry bit resulting from adding the three operands. A full adder may be used to add two B bit numbers by setting $A1$ and $A2$ to the least significant bits of the addends and setting $A3$ to 0. The resulting sum bit is the least significant bit of the answer. The resulting carry bit is used as the next value of $A3$, and the next bits of the addends are used as the values of $A1$ and $A2$. Repeating this process B times yields the desired sum. Two B bit numbers can be multiplied by performing, at most, $B - 1$ additions of shifted versions of the multiplicand and can be accomplished by using $B(B - 1)$ full adds.

Support for floating-point operations varies greatly. Some powerful custom processors include full floating-point support, while some bit-serial processors perform floating-point operations in software, one bit at a time. In between these extremes, some machines offer limited hardware support for floating-point operations, such as a barrel shifter, per processor, and others have standard floating-point coprocessors that are shared by several processors.

2.7 Selection of a Parallel Architecture

The best choice of a parallel architecture depends on the applications to be run, the programming model to be supported, and the costs to be considered. Distributed memory architectures typically offer better performance than shared memory architectures, because they improve the likelihood that a memory request can be satisfied locally. On the other hand, shared memory machines provide a separation between the processes that are running and the memory that they are accessing. As a result, load balancing can be accomplished in a shared memory architecture by moving processes from heavily loaded processors to lightly loaded ones. Load balancing is more difficult in a distributed memory architecture if the instruction set differentiates between accesses to local memory and to nonlocal memory. If such a differentiation exists, the local memory of a process must be moved with the process, thus, greatly increasing the overhead.

Although it might seem that shared memory architectures are better suited to providing the programmer with a high-level shared memory programming model, Chapter 3 will show that this is not necessarily the case.

Several shared memory architectures with small numbers of processors (fewer than 100) use busses to communicate between the processors and the memory. However, as the number of processors increases, bus-based systems usually become impractical. This is because a bus is typically connected to a large number of processors. Pin limitation (fan-out) considerations prevent any one processor from being connected to too many busses. Therefore, there are typically far fewer busses than processors, and a high bandwidth of communication cannot be supported. Busses may be useful if the application that is being solved involves far more computation than communication or if the communication that is required consists of broadcasting a small amount of data to a large number of locations. Also, several hybrid distributed memory architectures, with both busses and direct links between processors, have been proposed.[31,193,234] In these hybrid systems, the direct links are used to transfer large amounts of data between a small number of PEs, and the busses are used to transmit small amounts of data between large numbers of PEs.

The topology of the communication network is closely related to the applications that will be implemented. For example, a two-dimensional mesh interconnection supports low-level image processing applications very efficiently, while a hypercube interconnection supports symbolic, pointer-based data structures very well. The types of topologies that have been proposed and the applications that they support will be studied in detail in the following chapters.

The efficiency of SIMD or MIMD control is also very dependent on the application being implemented. For example, SIMD control is well-suited to those problems in which the granularity of computing is fine (that is, each PE is assigned only a few data items). An SIMD machine will perform efficiently in this case, since the small amount of data in each PE cannot have a rich structure, which could be exploited by an MIMD machine. In addition, the small amount of data per PE often indicates that the processing to be performed is intrinsically synchronous. Of course, SIMD control requires every processor to execute the same program, but this is a fairly common characteristic among numerical analysis and physics computations in which the PEs carry out a parallel algorithm cooperatively. In fact, even in some shared memory MIMD computers, an SPMD (single-program, multiple-data) paradigm has been proposed.[67] In this paradigm, a powerful coarse-grain MIMD architecture allows data-dependent processing to be performed efficiently.

By studying many examples from different application domains, it is seen that problems for which SIMD computing has been successfully used assign only a small number of data items to each PE. Specifically, the quantum-chromodynamics simulations carried out in the GF11 computer involve a few lattice points per processor;[19] in image processing operations,[156] each

PE handles a few image pixels;[1] in circuit simulations and layout optimization problems,[28,266] each processor handles a few devices, nets, or components; in parallel Fast Fourier Transform (FFT) algorithms,[183] each processor contains a sample of the signal; in sorting problems,[232] each PE typically holds one key.

Finally, the selection of a clocking scheme is very dependent on the other architecural decisions that have been made. For example, if SIMD control has been selected, then a single global clock is almost required. A single global clock may also be preferred because it provides a deterministic operation. On the other hand, the randomness caused by an asynchronous communication network could actually be desirable for performance reasons.[134]

---

[1] However, from a theoretical viewpoint, the product of the elapsed time and the number of processors may be improved significantly for some problems by using fewer processors.[8] In fact, in some cases, the elapsed time actually decreases when fewer processors are used.[161]

CHAPTER 3

High-Level Models

In this chapter, some of the different high-level models of parallel computers that have been proposed will be examined. A high-level model of a computer has two main purposes. First, it should simplify programming and algorithm design by providing a set of powerful, easy-to-compose, basic operations. Second, it should aid portability, so that a program or algorithm designed for one machine may be used on other machines. However, to be useful, it should accurately reflect the costs of the basic operations. This is essential because the wrong algorithm could be chosen if the costs of different algorithms cannot be accurately judged. The subject of high-level parallel models has been examined by other authors.[117,155,230]

High-level parallel models have been defined to capture the important features of both shared memory and distributed memory architectures. Although these high-level models are abstractions of particular architectures, it is important to realize that they are separate from the architectures. For example, it is possible to program a distributed memory architecture using a shared memory model. All that is required is systems software that implements the shared memory abstraction on the distributed memory hardware. This systems software is analogous to virtual memory support in a sequential machine, since in both cases, the software supports a model of the machine that is different from the underlying hardware. Similarly, it is possible to implement an SIMD model on MIMD hardware.[199]

3.1 Shared vs. Distributed Memory Models

3.1.1 Shared Memory Models

In a shared memory model,[128] there is a single global memory that all of the processors can access (write to or read from) in unit time. In addition to the global shared memory, each processor has a local private memory in which data and pointers to the global memory may be stored.

The most popular shared memory model is the PRAM (parallel random access machine).[33,128] There are a number of variants of the PRAM model, each with a different policy for handling multiple simultaneous accesses to a single global memory location. The most restrictive PRAM model is the EREW (exclusive read, exclusive write) PRAM. In an EREW PRAM, no two processors are allowed to read from or write to a single global memory location at the same time. It is the programmer's responsibility to ensure that such simultaneous reads and writes do not occur. In a CREW (concurrent read, exclusive write) PRAM, multiple processors may read a single global memory location simultaneously, but no two processors can write to the same memory location at the same time. Finally, in a CRCW (concurrent read, concurrent write) PRAM, multiple processors may read from or write to a single global memory location simultaneously.

The class of CRCW PRAMs may be further subdivided by examining their implementation of concurrent writes. In a COMMON CRCW PRAM, simultaneous writes are only allowed if all of the processors writing to a single memory location are writing the same value. In an ARBITRARY CRCW PRAM, simultaneous writes to a single location cause one of the values being written to that location to be stored. However, the selection of which value is stored is made arbitrarily. In a PRIORITY CRCW PRAM, simultaneous writes to a single memory location result in the value from the lowest numbered processor that is writing to the location being stored.

In a retrospective analysis, it can be seen that the PRAM model is an abstraction of the multistage switch-based architectures. Furthermore, the different types of PRAM models arise from the known concerns about traffic congestion and "hot spots" in multistage networks.[186] The PRAM model has been embraced very strongly by the theory community, and consequently, many algorithms for important problems are known for this programming model only.

3.1.2 Distributed Memory Models

Distributed memory models are abstractions of processor-based, distributed memory architectures. Each processor in a distributed memory model can access its own local memory in unit time, but access to data in other processors' local memories requires additional time for communicating the data. In a distributed memory model, certain pairs of processors are connected by direct communication links. Only processors that have a communication link connecting them are allowed to communicate, and at most one data item may be transferred in a given direction on a given communication link in unit time. Some distributed memory models allow data to be transferred in both directions along a communication link simultaneously, while others require that data be transferred in one direction at a time.

As was the case with processor-based machines, distributed memory models may be categorized by the type of communication that they support. Some models, called *strong communication* models, allow a single processor to send a different data item over each of its communication links in unit time. Other models, called *weak communication* models, limit each processor to sending a single data item over a single communication link at a time.

Shared memory models are generally easier to program than distributed memory models. This is because shared memory models allow the programmer to ignore the communication costs and to concentrate on the division of the problem into tasks that can be performed in parallel. Furthermore, there are only a few different types of shared memory models, and the different types are very closely related. For example, an algorithm designed for an EREW PRAM will perform equally well on a CREW PRAM or an ARBITRARY CRCW PRAM. On the other hand, there are many different interconnection topologies for distributed memory models, and an algorithm designed for a model with one interconnection topology might run poorly on a machine with a different interconnection topology. Because of these advantages, the shared memory models, in general, and the PRAM models, in particular, have been very popular with parallel algorithm designers. However, there are many arguments for both the shared memory and the distributed memory models. Some of these arguments are considered next.

3.1.2 Accuracy of the Models

The fact that shared memory models hide communication costs can be a serious problem. Communication is often more expensive than computation in real parallel machines. However, the PRAM model assumes a unit cost for a parallel memory access, regardless of the number of processors in the machine. No actual machine can provide this sort of performance when accessing a shared memory. As a result, the PRAM model can give a misleading view of the efficiency of a parallel algorithm. In contrast, distributed memory models can be quite accurate in predicting the running time of a program on a processor-based architecture. The distributed memory model has been used by many authors because communication costs are believed to be of major importance in parallel computing.[155,174,230]

An even more serious difficulty with shared memory models is that they may force the programmer to create suboptimal algorithms. A high-level programming model should guide the programmer to efficient algorithms. Snyder has given several examples of problems for which the PRAM algorithms, when implemented on an actual machine, are slower than the distributed memory algorithms for the same problems.[230] In particular, Snyder has shown that the best PRAM algorithms for maximum selection and for successive overrelaxation (SOR) lead to suboptimal implementations. The key problem with the PRAM is that it hides from the user the way in which communication is implemented. If a PRAM algorithm has time complexity $C(P)$, and even if a cost of accessing memory $F(P)$ were disclosed to the programmer, little could be done in the program to avoid a resulting algorithm with complexity $F(P)*C(P)$. This feature is, in fact, what lies at the heart of the criticism given by Snyder,[230] in which the performance of maximum selection and SOR algorithms is analyzed.

The two examples given by Snyder use structured, data-independent patterns of communication. Specifically, the SOR algorithm requires only local communication in a two-dimensional grid, while the maximum computation can be accomplished by using a tree structure. It is natural that structured, data-independent patterns of communication can be implemented more efficiently when the topology of the computer is known to the algorithm designer. By knowing both the communication pattern and the interconnection topology, the algorithm designer can tailor the algorithm to match the architecture. An interesting question that these examples cannot answer is whether there is any algorithm that involves highly *irregular* communication among PEs and still has better performance when designed for a distributed memory model. The answer is affirmative, as will be demonstrated in Sections 10.10 and 11.7 by several algorithms that are based on the strategy of reducing the amount of data prior to performing irregular communication.[213]

3.1.2 Portability of the Models

Interestingly, it has been claimed that the major advantage of the PRAM is that it provides portable programs. Furthermore, in the theory community; it is widely believed that simulating PRAMs is the only way to reconcile "ideal" parallel computing models with "real" machines. Neither of these remarks is fully correct.

The lack of generality of distributed memory algorithms is actually less serious than it might appear. Although many different topologies have been proposed for distributed memory computers, many of these topologies are related. Therefore, classes of parallel algorithms may be defined that run efficiently on many different distributed memory machines. An example of such a class consists of algorithms for the hypercube and several constant degree topologies related to the hypercube, which will be presented in Chapter 9. Languages for distributed memory models should offer a large set of communication routines forming a library of tools for programming. These routines should capture the communication characteristics of many algorithms and be fairly independent of the particular interconnection network. Of course, the efficiency of their implementation will ultimately hinge upon the topology of the network, but programs written in this style should be completely portable.

Simulating PRAMs can be a very inefficient technique for reconciling real and idealized programming models. The PRAM is an MIMD model. However, the communication schemes used in most of today's MIMD computers cannot support PRAM algorithms efficiently. Some reasons are the overhead introduced by the operating system, unnecessary buffering, and handshaking.[258] These factors become severe bottlenecks because a PRAM simulation will involve many short messages (typically consisting of a few bytes). Furthermore, the PRAM is a synchronous model, and most existing MIMD computers are asynchronous. Therefore, the synchronization costs required for simulating a PRAM can also be prohibitive.

Despite its limitations, the PRAM model is a convenient one for "naive" programmers. Not all users will have the sophisticated skills necessary to exploit the peculiar characteristics of computing problems and parallel machines. In fact, even programming in the PRAM style is far from being trivial. Devising highly parallel algorithms is difficult, regardless of the programming model and the language. Also, there will be some problems for which the extra cost incurred in using the PRAM will not be a reason for dismissal. Thus, it would be best to have a computer architecture that can support both the shared and distributed memory models reasonably efficiently. Unfortunately, the currently available parallel computers do not provide efficient implementations of both models. Some existing switch-based parallel computers implement a shared memory model, but they cannot be programmed more efficiently with a distributed memory model. On the other hand, existing distributed memory MIMD computers cannot provide an efficient shared memory abstraction or an efficient implementation of algorithms with regular, data-independent communication patterns.

3.2 Synchronous vs. Asynchronous Models

Another important distinction is whether a high-level parallel model is synchronous or asynchronous. In a synchronous parallel model, there is a single global clock that regulates all of the processors in the machine. In contrast, in an asynchronous model, the processors operate at different speeds, and the order in which different tasks are completed is not guaranteed. Asynchronous models typically provide primitives for coordinating the activities of different processors. For example, a barrier synchronization operation may be provided that causes each processor to wait until the remaining processors reach the same synchronization point. Also, a locking mechanism may be provided, which guarantees that only one processor will access a shared memory location at a time.

The primary advantage of asynchronous models over synchronous ones is that they can offer improved performance, because they do not have to make worst case assumptions about the completion times of instructions. Instructions can require different amounts of time in different processors for a number of reasons. For example, simple instructions, such as fixed-point additions, are faster than complex ones, such as floating-point divisions. Also, some processors may be operating on data that are stored in local memory, while others may be processing remotely stored data. Finally, even if all processors are accessing remote data, variations in congestion and contention in the communication network can lead to different instruction times.

Although asynchronous models have a performance advantage when instruction times vary, there are several inefficiencies that are unique to asynchronous models. When several processors access a single data structure in an asynchronous model, the programmer must add explicit instructions to avoid updating the data structure in an inconsistent manner. For example, a semaphore could be used to guarantee that only one processor accesses the structure at a time. The use of a semaphore increases the number of remote accesses that each processor must perform.

Semaphores and other synchronization variables are also likely to create hot spots in the communication network, which can seriously degrade performance. Combining networks have been proposed to handle such hot spots.[186] Combining networks are switch-based networks in which multiple requests to a single memory location are merged when they meet one another in a switch. One proposed combining network would implement the "fetch-and-add" family of operations.[96] A fetch-and-add operation is an atomic operation that adds a given value to a specified variable and returns the updated value. When two fetch-and-add operations destined for the same variable meet in a switch, they are merged and a request to increase the variable by the sum of the original requests is forwarded. The fetch-and-add requests to a single memory location, thus, form a tree that is rooted at that memory location. The updated results of the fetch-and-add are then broadcast back from the memory to the processors along this tree.

Fetch-and-add operations are of great value in scheduling processes and in supporting other system software features needed in general purpose computing environments. However, recent research suggests that deterministic versions of the fetch-and-add primitives, such as multiple-parallel-prefix, are more powerful.[200] Perhaps these new deterministic constructs will be better able to control the potential randomness in signal processing, numerical algebra, partial differential equations (PDEs) and image analysis applications, but this remains to be demonstrated.

While asynchrony is of potential benefit in parallel algorithms, it has been, by and large, a source of troubles. Asynchronous models are extremely difficult to program, debug, or analyze. Because many orderings of operations are possible when executing an asynchronous program, it is difficult to compose operations and subroutines to obtain the desired behavior. Debugging asynchronous programs ranges from difficult to impossible, since they can produce different outputs from a single input. Because there is no concept of the state of an asynchronous model, reasoning about asynchronous programs can be very difficult. Also, the lack of a global concept of time makes it difficult to define the time requirements of an algorithm or to analyze which algorithm for a given problem is the fastest.

In contrast, synchronous models are generally easier to program, analyze, and debug than asynchronous models. This is because synchronous models advance through a deterministic sequence of states. Thus, the length of this sequence of states can be taken as a measure of the time requirements of the program. Furthermore, because the behavior of a synchronous model is determined solely by its program and its input, a synchronous program can be debugged by stepping through its states. As a result of these differences, the synchronous models have been favored by algorithm designers. For example, the PRAM models described earlier are all synchronous models. An illuminating discussion of the relative merits of synchronous and asynchronous machines has been presented by P. Gibbons.[94]

Asynchronous MIMD models have been used for problems that could be solved simply in a synchronous SIMD model. The resulting programs are difficult to write, cumbersome to read, and nearly impossible to debug. These problems have become so obvious that a recent research publication has been devoted to showing that "MIMD software is in a sorry state."[126] Asynchrony is an unnecessary trouble unless it is conclusively proven that a problem has to make use of it. Although general purpose parallel computers should definitely support an asynchronous MIMD computing style, this style is obviously not necessary for innumerable specific applications. Although a few constructive uses of asynchrony have been shown[68,102,140,134] today's major consumers of parallelism do not require asynchronous MIMD models, and hence, the "sorry state" of MIMD software should not have any impact on these users.

3.3 Synchronized Communication Models

The performance of synchronous models is limited by the frequent synchronization operations, while asynchronous models are nondeterministic and difficult to program. A promising compromise between these two models is given by the *synchronized communication* (SC) models. In an SC model, an algorithm consists of successive phases in which either computations or communications are performed. These two phases are well-distinguished in the sense that they never occur at the same time. If processor control is distributed, some synchronization is necessary before a communication phase starts. Communication is handled entirely by the PEs by executing instructions stored in their own memory or broadcast by a single controller. Because processors only interact with one another by communicating, SC models are deterministic and guarantee the same output given a single input. The SC model generalizes the compute-aggregate-broadcast (CAB) paradigm presented by Nelson and Snyder.[174]

The distinction between synchronized and asynchronous communication is relevant to all aspects of parallel computing. The impact of this choice on hardware, software, and the performance and analysis of algorithms is considerable. Past research also supports this view.[140,155]

An SC model may have either shared or distributed memory. The shared memory version is identical to the asynchronous PRAM model introduced by Gibbons.[94] In a distributed SC model, it is natural to use a processor-based, rather than a switch-based, implementation. This is because the processors are not performing computations when communication is occurring, so they would be idle in a switch-based architecture.

All SIMD models are necessarily SC models, but MIMD SC models are also possible. The issue of processor control autonomy is not as important as processor synchronization during the communication phase. In other words, it does not really matter whether all processors execute the same instruction, as long as the instructions do not involve communication. When an operation does involve communication, the processors will cooperatively perform the necessary steps to accomplish it in a synchronized manner.

The validity of a computing model is ultimately established by showing the way algorithms make use of it. Synchronized communication is applicable to a wide variety of parallel computing problems.[28,86,104,106,118,166,183,221] Many algorithms have appeared in the literature for SIMD computing, all of which fall within the SC model. More surprisingly, many algorithms developed for MIMD computers also fall within this model. Perhaps this characteristic has remained hidden by the nature of the asynchronous MIMD computers used to run the algorithms.

CHAPTER 4

Mesh Connected Computers

4.1 Introduction to Mesh Connected Computers

A d-dimensional mesh computer is a processor-based distributed memory parallel computer in which the processing elements (PEs) are arranged in a d-dimensional cube. Each PE is connected to its two neighbors in each of the d dimensions, if they exist. Two-dimensional mesh computers are particularly important (see Figure 4.1), but three-dimensional meshes have also been built.[175] Each PE consists of a processor and an associated memory. Here, the focus will be on two-dimensional meshes (which are simply called "mesh connected computers") that operate in an SIMD mode.

A mesh connected computer is easy to construct because it is regular, it has short connections, it requires only four connections per PE, and it is possible to build in two dimensions without having any connections cross. Each PE that is not on an edge of the array has a direct connection with its four nearest neighbors. The edge PEs can either be connected to a smaller number of PEs or to the corresponding PEs on the opposite edge. In the latter case, the top row is connected to the bottom row and the leftmost column is connected to the rightmost column, so the interconnections logically form a torus. The construction of such a machine in two dimensions requires that some connections cross.

I/O operations in a mesh connected computer are typically performed one column (or row) at a time. This simplifies the connections between the array of PEs and the external memory or I/O devices. For instance, in one design, only the leftmost column has I/O connections. A new set of data can be loaded by moving the rightmost column of data in parallel into the leftmost column of the array. Then, this column of data is shifted one column to the right, while the next column of data is entering the array. The process of shifting the data one column to the right and loading a new column into the array is repeated until the entire data set has been loaded. Thus, the loading of N data items into an N processor machine can be accomplished with $N^{1/2}$ shift operations. Some mesh connected computers allow I/O operations to be

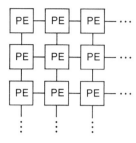

Fig. 4.1. Mesh connected computer.

performed simultaneously, and some allow I/O and data processing operations to be performed simultaneously.

In addition to the mesh array structure described above, there are three important extensions that are often implemented or proposed. The first extension is the inclusion of a tree of OR gates that calculates the logical OR of a certain 1-bit register located in each PE. The output of this tree of OR gates is 1 if any of the PEs contains a 1 in the specified register, and, otherwise, is 0. The output of the tree is available to the control unit and can be used to terminate repetitive operations in a data-dependent manner. For instance, an algorithm may require that a local neighborhood operation be performed on all pixels until all of the pixels attain a stable value. If no such tree of OR gates is present, the determination of whether or not any values have changed on the last iteration is a very time-consuming process. As a result, it may be best to perform the operation a fixed number of times, such as the maximum number required for convergence. With the tree of OR gates, however, it is possible to perform only as many iterations as are actually required.

The second extension is a tree of additional processors that can be used to extract global information from the array of PEs. One use of such a tree is to quickly count the number of pixels that have a certain value, thus, speeding the generation of a histogram. Many other uses will be shown later.

The third extension is an ability to reconfigure the mesh connections so that a value sent along a single mesh connection is propagated along additional mesh connections.[105,153,154] As a result, entire regions of processors can exchange data as if they were connected by a bus that is accessible to all of them. The reconfiguration of the mesh connections can be dependent on the data stored in the processors, so they can be set to match the properties of an image. For example, if each region of connected processors corresponds to an object in an image, the reconfigured mesh connections can aid in the computation of properties of the objects.

While the above description provides a simple, idealized model of mesh connected computers, no actual computer matches the model exactly. The next four sections examine several mesh connected SIMD computers that have been built, namely the CLIP4, the GAPP, the MPP, and the MasPar MP-1. Special attention is given to the unique characteristics of each. Chapter 5 analyzes algorithms for performing a number of image processing tasks on mesh connected computers.

4.2 CLIP4

The cellular logic image processor (CLIP4) is a mesh connected computer designed specifically for image processing. CLIP4 was built at the University College, London, under the direction of M. J. B. Duff. It was completed in 1980, and it consists of 9,216 PEs arranged in a 96 X 96 array. Each PE has a bit-serial processor and 32 bits of memory. Custom NMOS LSI chips were created, each of which contains eight processors and their associated memory. The memory is located on-chip because inexpensive RAM chips were not available when the machine was designed. The processors operate in an SIMD mode with uniform addressing. Each chip contains 4,000 devices and has 40 pins. The chips operate with a 400-ns clock cycle. CLIP4 can be programmed with a parallel version of the C language. The interested reader can find CLIP4 hardware information in Refs. 72 and 74 and programming information in Refs. 50 and 73.

The design of the processor is shown in Fig. 4.2. All data lines in the figure are 1 bit wide. The box labeled D contains the processor's 32 bits of memory.

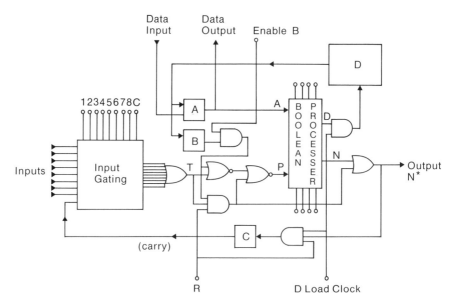

Fig. 4.2. CLIP4 processor design [Duff, 1978].

Memory addresses are sent from the control unit, so CLIP4 uses uniform addressing. There are three 1-bit registers labeled A, B, and C. An image may be shifted in or out of the array by using the lines marked "data input" and "data output." The partially shifted image is stored in the A registers of the array. The A register may also be loaded from the memory registers and can be used as an input to the boolean processor. The B register is loaded from the memory registers and can be used as an input to the processor. The C register contains the carry bit during bit-serial additions and multiplications. The processor has two independent outputs: one to the memory registers and one to the neighboring PEs. The processor has eight control lines and is capable of performing all of the 2^8 binary functions from two inputs to two outputs. There are no mask registers in CLIP4, although the effect of having mask registers can be simulated by performing additional boolean operations.

It is also possible to use the processor as a full adder of the registers A, B, and C. In terms of the diagram in Fig. 4.2, the processor calculates $N = P$ AND A and $D = P$ XOR A, the control line labeled R is set to TRUE, and the input gating is set so that $T = C$. With this setting, the D output of the boolean processor is the sum bit and the input to the C register is the carry bit.

Each PE is physically connected to each of its eight nearest neighbors via a 1-bit-wide connection. By disabling some of the physical connections, the control unit can specify a logical interconnection network in which each PE is connected to six neighbors. In this manner, a hexagonal array of PEs can be simulated. Each PE can access any subset of its six or eight neighbors in parallel. The inputs from all of the accessed neighbors are ORed together and combined with the A and B registers as an input to the boolean processor. There are no connections between the edges of the array, therefore, a toroidal interconnection network is not supported. In addition to the eight input links already described, each PE has a single data input link connected to the A register that allows for fast I/O operations. Because both I/O and data processing operations use the A register, it is impossible to perform I/O and data processing operations simultaneously. A special feature of CLIP4 is a tree of adders that has one of the columns of 96 PEs at its base. The adders are used to speed the totalization of data in the array. The output of the tree of adders is available to the central controller.

The controller is a special processor that is external to the array of PEs. It fetches instructions from its private memory, decodes them, and broadcasts commands to all of the processors in the array. The controller instructions contain either 16 or 32 bits. The controller has 14 general purpose 16-bit registers. It also has a special purpose 16-bit register that holds the output of the tree of adders described earlier. Each instruction has a bit that specifies whether the missing neighbors of the edge PEs provide a 0 or a 1 to the edge PEs.

As described earlier, I/O operations are performed by shifting one column of data in or out at a time. The special data input and output lines allow a

96×96 binary image to be loaded in 4 ms. Binary images that are to be loaded into the array are first placed in a 9,216-bit shift register that is external to the array. This shift register is then reconfigured into 96 shift registers of 96 bits each, and the image is shifted into the array from these shift registers. A binary image is removed from the array by reversing the above procedure. An n-bit gray level image is loaded into the array by repeating the loading procedure for a binary image n times.

There are no provisions in CLIP4 for fault tolerance. If any of the nearly 10,000 processors fails, it must be replaced before regular operations can continue. This could be a serious problem because of the large number of processors. Fortunately, the processors are all identical, therefore, it is sufficient to keep a small number of extra processor chips to be used as replacements.

The most important special features of CLIP4 are the tree of adders and the ability to access any subset of a PE's eight nearest neighbors in parallel. The tree of adders is connected to only one column of the array, so 96 shift operations are required to move all pixels to the tree. While a tree of adders with connections to all of the pixels would count pixels considerably faster, the small tree present in the CLIP4 is still useful. The ability to access eight neighbors in parallel reduces the time required to perform some local neighborhood operations. The most significant shortcoming of CLIP4 is the limited memory size (32 bits per PE). Another shortcoming is the lack of a tree of OR gates, which would allow the controller to perform a loop in a data-dependent manner. These shortcomings are understandable in a machine that was begun in 1973, before inexpensive RAM was available and before any other large, mesh connected computers had been built.

4.3 GAPP

The **g**eometric **a**rithmetic **p**arallel **p**rocessor (GAPP) is the first commercial chip for a mesh connected, image processing computer. The chip was built in 1984 in a joint project between NCR and Martin Marietta under the direction of Sullivan, Thomas, and Holsztynski. The chip was designed for image processing and pattern recognition applications. Unlike CLIP4 and the MPP, GAPP is not a complete computer because it does not include a controller and a buffer memory through which I/O operations can be performed. Instead, it is a set of PEs that can be used in a mesh connected computer of arbitrary size. NCR does provide a small complete computer containing four GAPP chips, but any size array is conceivable. The four-chip board comes with software that provides a high-level interface to the processors. Each GAPP chip contains 72 bit-serial processors, each of which has 128 bits of memory located on the chip. The chip was implemented in CMOS using three micron design rules. Each chip has 84 pins and can operate with a 100-ns clock cycle. GAPP operates in an SIMD mode with uniform addressing and communication. Information on GAPP may be found in Ref. 172.

The layout of a single PE is shown in Figure 4.3. All data lines in the figure are 1 bit wide, as are the registers CM (**c**ommunications), NS (**n**orth-**s**outh), EW (**e**ast-**w**est), and C (**c**arry). The instruction set is shown in Fig. 4.4 and the processor operations are shown in Fig. 4.5. As can be seen from Fig. 4.5,

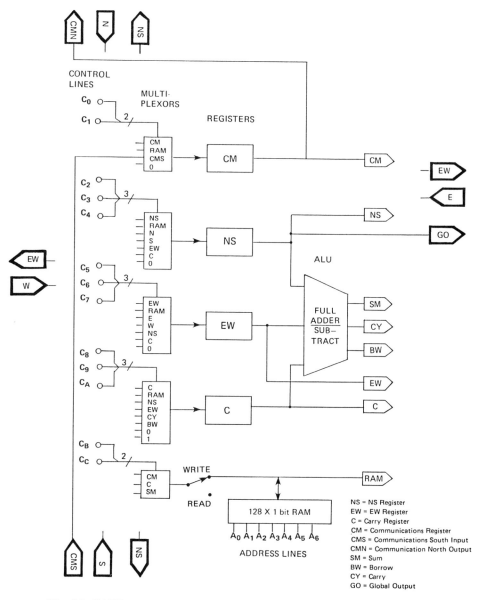

Fig. 4.3. GAPP processor [NCR Microelectronic Products Division, 1984].

Register Operation	Mnemonic	C_C	C_B	C_A	C_9	C_8	C_7	C_6	C_5	C_4	C_3	C_2	C_1	C_0	Description
	CM: = CM	X	X	X	X	X	X	X	X	X	X	X	0	0	MICRO-NOP
CM	CM: = RAM	X	X	X	X	X	X	X	X	X	X	X	0	1	LOAD CM FROM RAM
	CM: = CMS	X	X	X	X	X	X	X	X	X	X	X	1	0	MOVE FROM CMS INTO CM
	CM: =0	X	X	X	X	X	X	X	X	X	X	X	1	1	LOAD 0 INTO CM
	NS: = NS	X	X	X	X	X	X	X	X	0	0	0	X	X	MICRO-NOP
	NS: = RAM	X	X	X	X	X	X	X	X	0	0	1	X	X	LOAD NS FROM RAM
	NS: = N	X	X	X	X	X	X	X	X	0	1	0	X	X	MOVE FROM N INTO NS
NS	NS: = S	X	X	X	X	X	X	X	X	0	1	1	X	X	MOVE FROM S INTO NS
	NS: = EW	X	X	X	X	X	X	X	X	1	0	0	X	X	MOVE FROM EW INTO NS
	NS: = C	X	X	X	X	X	X	X	X	1	0	1	X	X	MOVE FROM C INTO NS
	NS: =0	X	X	X	X	X	X	X	X	1	1	0	X	X	LOAD 0 INTO NS
	EW: = EW	X	X	X	X	X	0	0	0	X	X	X	X	X	MICRO-NOP
	EW: = RAM	X	X	X	X	X	0	0	1	X	X	X	X	X	LOAD EW FROM RAM
	EW: = E	X	X	X	X	X	0	1	0	X	X	X	X	X	MOVE FROM E INTO EW
EW	EW: = W	X	X	X	X	X	0	1	1	X	X	X	X	X	MOVE FROM W INTO EW
	EW: = NS	X	X	X	X	X	1	0	0	X	X	X	X	X	MOVE FROM NS INTO EW
	EW: = C	X	X	X	X	X	1	0	1	X	X	X	X	X	MOVE FROM C INTO EW
	EW: =0	X	X	X	X	X	1	1	0	X	X	X	X	X	LOAD 0 INTO EW
	C: = C	X	X	0	0	0	X	X	X	X	X	X	X	X	MICRO-NOP
	C: = RAM	X	X	0	0	1	X	X	X	X	X	X	X	X	LOAD C FROM RAM
	C: = NS	X	X	0	1	0	X	X	X	X	X	X	X	X	MOVE FROM NS INTO C
C	C: = EW	X	X	0	1	1	X	X	X	X	X	X	X	X	MOVE FROM EW INTO C
	C: = CY	X	X	1	0	0	X	X	X	X	X	X	X	X	LOAD C FROM CARRY
	C: = BW	X	X	1	0	1	X	X	X	X	X	X	X	X	LOAD C FROM BORROW
	C: =0	X	X	1	1	0	X	X	X	X	X	X	X	X	LOAD 0 INTO C
	C: =1	X	X	1	1	1	X	X	X	X	X	X	X	X	LOAD 1 INTO C
	READ	0	0	X	X	X	X	X	X	X	X	X	X	X	READ FROM RAM
RAM	RAM: = CM	0	1	X	X	X	X	X	X	X	X	X	X	X	LOAD RAM FROM CM
	RAM: = C	1	0	X	X	X	X	X	X	X	X	X	X	X	LOAD RAM FROM C
	RAM: = SM	1	1	X	X	X	X	X	X	X	X	X	X	X	LOAD RAM FROM SUM

Fig. 4.4. GAPP instruction set [NCR Microelectronic Products Division, 1984].

Adder/Subtracter Operations

INPUT			OUTPUT		
NS	EW	C	SM	CY	BW
0	0	0	0	0	0
0	1	0	1	0	1
1	0	0	1	0	0
1	1	0	0	1	0
0	0	1	1	0	1
0	1	1	0	1	1
1	0	1	0	1	0
1	1	1	1	1	1

LOGICAL OPERATION	DESCRIPTION	CONDITIONS
INV	$SM = \overline{NS}$	EW = 0, C = 1
	$SM = \overline{EW}$	NS = 0, C = 1
	$SM = \overline{C}$	NS = 0, EW = 1
AND	$CY = NS \bullet EW$	C = 0
	$CY = EW \bullet C$	NS = 0
	$CY = NS \bullet C$	EW = 0
	$BW = \overline{NS} \bullet EW$	C = 0
OR	$CY = NS + EW$	C = 1
	$BW = \overline{NS} + EW$	C = 1
	$BW = EW + C$	NS = 0
XOR	$SM = NS \oplus C$	EW = 0
	$SM = NS \oplus EW$	C = 0
	$SM = EW \oplus C$	NS = 0
XNOR	$SM = \overline{NS} \oplus \overline{EW}$	C = 1

Fig. 4.5. GAPP processor operation [NCR Microelectronic Products Division, 1984].

the processor may be used as a full adder. Also, it can perform a small number of other boolean functions of three inputs, which facilitate subtractions, but it cannot perform all of the possible boolean functions of three arguments. The inputs to the full adder are the NS, EW, and C registers. The outputs are labeled SM (sum), CY (carry), and BW (borrow). The SM and CY outputs are the sum and carry bits of the full adder. The BW output is the carry bit resulting from the addition of EW, C, and the inverse of NS. Integer addition is performed in a bit-serial manner using the full adder, exactly as in CLIP4. Integer subtraction is performed identically, except the BW output is used instead of the CY output, and the C input is initialized to 1. This performs the addition of the number, which is loaded 1 bit at a time into the EW register, with the 2s-complement of the number placed in the NS register. GAPP processors do not have mask registers.

The CM register is used for I/O operations. It can be loaded from the CM register of the processor immediately to the south (below) or from the RAM. The NS register can be loaded from the NS register of the processor immediately to the north or south, from the EW or C register of the same processor, or from RAM. The EW register can be loaded from the EW register of the processor immediately to the east or west, from the NS or C register of the same processor, or from RAM. The C register can be loaded from the NS or EW register of the same processor, from the CY or BW outputs of the full adder, from RAM, or it can be set to 1. In addition to the possibilities listed above, all four registers can be left unchanged or cleared to 0. The RAM can be read from or written to by the C or CM register or by the SM output of the full adder. All four registers and the RAM have separate control lines and can be set independently of one another. In particular, it is possible to perform I/O shifting while performing arithmetic or logical operations. As in the other mesh connected machines, I/O operations are performed by shifting the image one row or column at a time.

The network is a square mesh with each PE connected to its four nearest neighbors. Because the GAPP is only a chip, it could be used in a toroidal configuration if the proper connections were added between PEs at the edge of the array. All data transfers occur one bit at a time, with all PEs communicating with the same set of neighbors at any one time. Each chip provides a GO (global output) line, which is the OR of the NS registers of the 72 PEs on the chip. This is provided so that a tree of OR gates connecting all of the PEs can be used by the controller for data-dependent loops. There is no provision for fault tolerance within the chip, but it would be possible to use extra chips in an array of chips to provide fault tolerance. Such a system will be described in the MPP section.

The most significant strengths of the GAPP chip are the large number of processors per chip (72) and the global output line for calculating the OR of a specific register from all of the PEs in the array. The greatest weaknesses are the limited capabilities of the processors and the small amount of memory per processor (128 bits).

4.4 The MPP

The massively parallel processor (MPP) was completed in 1983 under the direction of Kenneth Batcher. The MPP was created at Goodyear Aerospace under a contract from the NASA Goddard Space Flight Center. It is a truly massive machine, containing 16K bit-serial PEs arranged in a 128 × 128 square mesh. It operates in an SIMD mode, with uniform addressing and communication, under the direction of a number of specially designed controllers. Each PE contains 1,024 bits of memory, giving the machine a total of 16 Mbits of memory. The array of PEs consists of custom chips, each of which contains eight processors. The chips are implemented with HCMOS using 5 micron design rules. Each chip has 8,000 devices and 52 pins. The PE's memory is located off chip. The MPP can be programmed using a parallel version of Pascal. Additional information on the MPP can be found in Refs. 17, 70, 141, 189, and 190.

The layout of a single MPP PE is shown in Fig. 4.6. Each PE has one I/O register (called the S register), five 1-bit processing registers (called A, B, C, G and P), and one 30-bit shift register. Logic operations use the P register as one input and either another register, a local memory value, or a value from the P register in one of the four nearest neighbors as the second input. Any of the 16 possible boolean functions of 2 arguments can be calculated. The result is placed in the P register.

The P register is also used for arithmetic operations. There is a full adder that takes as input registers A, P, and C and places the sum bit in B and the carry bit in C. The shift register can also be used in arithmetic operations. It takes the contents of register B as input and can optionally place the shifted out bit in register A. The physical length of the shift register is 30 bits, but its logical length can be set from 2 to 30 bits in increments of 4 bits. The shift register is used for performing bit-serial arithmetic operations without accessing RAM.

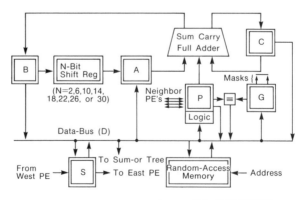

Fig. 4.6. MPP processor layout [© 1982 IEEE].

The G register is a mask register. Most operations have two modes: masked and unmasked. Unmasked operations operate on all processors, while masked ones operate only on the PEs that have 1s in their G registers. The arithmetic operations and the logic operations can be specified as masked or unmasked independently of one another. However, both arithmetic and logic operations use the G register for determining the mask value.

The S register is used for I/O shifting. It can be loaded from either the local memory or the S register of the neighbor to the left. Its output can be placed either in local memory or the S register of the neighbor to the right. The operation of the S register is independent of the other processing operations, and I/O may be performed in parallel with processing, except when the local memory is accessed.

The PEs are arranged in a square mesh with each PE directly connected to its four nearest neighbors. Logically, the array is a square of 128×128 PEs, but physically, it has 132 columns of 128 PEs each. The extra four columns are provided so that a defective chip can be isolated by disabling the column of chips to which it belongs. A disabled column of chips simply passes signals between the columns to its left and right. Thus, the chips to the left and right are unaware of the change. Although a defective and disabled chip must still perform the function of transferring data between its neighbors, the circuitry to perform this function is very simple and is unlikely to be defective. As a result, the majority of single-chip defects can be isolated without any inconvenience to an applications programmer.

The edges of the mesh may be left unconnected, connected and aligned, or connected and offset by 1 PE. These options allow for a square, a vertical and a horizontal cylinder, a torus, a linear array (which spirals through the PEs), and a loop (which also spirals through the PEs). The connection options are shown in Fig. 4.7. All PEs must access the same neighbor during a single instruction, and only one neighbor may be accessed at a time. Data transfers between neighbors move 1 bit of data in one instruction cycle (100 ns). In addition to the data connections already described, there is a set of horizontal nearest-neighbor connections for performing I/O operations. There is also a set of trees of OR gates, called the SUM-OR trees, which provide the control unit with the OR of a specific register in the PEs. The array of PEs is logically divided into 8 groups of 16 rows each, with each group having its own SUM-OR tree. The SUM-OR trees can be used to terminate an iterative process in a data-dependent manner. Also, there is a network for transferring bits from 16 evenly spaced PEs, which are called the "corners." If the PEs are numbered $(0, \ldots, 127, 0, \ldots, 127)$, then the corners are the PEs (i, j) such that $i = 31 \bmod 32$ and $j = 31 \bmod 32$. The connections to the corners reduce the amount of time required to move small amounts of data from the array to the controller. For instance, the number of pixels with a value of 1 in a binary image can be calculated by counting the number of 1s in each 32×32 window and then sending the results to the controller by using the connections from the corners.

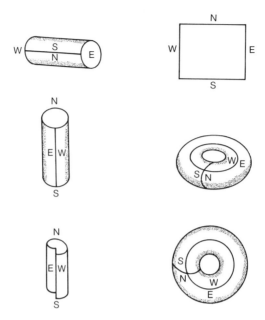

Fig. 4.7. MPP connection options [© 1982 IEEE].

Each PE has 1,024 bits of local RAM. Four processors share one 1K × 4 RAM chip. All processors must access the same memory location on each instruction. Each memory plane (a single memory location in all PEs) of 16K bits contains 2,048 parity bits for error detection. These parity bits may be enabled or disabled by the programmer. The memory can be accessed more quickly (in 100 ns) when the parity generation and checking is disabled. The parity error indicators can be used as the input to the SUM-OR trees so that the control unit can detect a RAM error.

Images that will be transferred to the array of PEs or that have just been removed from the array are held in a buffer called the staging memory. The staging memory contains four bank, each of which holds 64K 64-bit words. Provisions have been made so that the staging memory can be expanded to 32 banks of 1M 64-bit words as memory technology improves. The staging memory is capable of a wide range of reformatting operations. For instance, most external devices represent a gray level image as a single array of 8-bit words. This representation must be converted into eight arrays of 1-bit words, so that it can be loaded efficiently into the array of PEs. The staging memory can perform this reformatting very quickly. Another type of re-formatting that can be performed by the staging memory is the accessing of every fourth row and column of a 512 × 512 image so that it will fit in the 128 × 128 array of PEs.

The MPP controller is external to the processors and consists of three parts: the main control unit (MCU), the processing element control unit (PECU), and the input/output control unit (IOCU). The MCU coordinates the activity of the other control units and performs all scalar operations. The MCU has 50 16-bit registers. Of these registers, 16 are general purpose, 3 specify which 4 of the 132 physical columns of processors are disabled for fault tolerance, 1 contains the output of the SUM-OR trees, and the remainder are used for communication with the PECU and IOCU and for status information. The MCU issues commands to the PECU by placing them in a 16-element FIFO queue.

The PECU is the unit that directly controls the array of PEs. It takes a command from the MCU and responds by performing an entire routine of operations that is stored in its private memory. The PECU has a subroutine stack, therefore, a routine called by the MCU can call another routine, which can, in turn, call another. The PECU also contains eight 16-bit index registers, a 64-bit common register, a 3-bit topology register, a program counter, and an instruction register. The index registers are used for addressing memory locations and holding loop variables. The common register holds scalar values and can receive the contents of the 16 corner memory elements and the output of the SUM-OR trees (both of which were described earlier). The topology register controls the connections between processors on the edges of the array. Parameters for PECU routines can be passed from the MCU to the PECU in the index registers and the common register, and the contents of the common register can be passed back to the MCU.

The IOCU performs I/O subroutines that either shift the contents of the processors' S registers a given number of columns or transfer data between the S registers and RAM. The staging memory is usually controlled by a VAX 11/780 host computer. The MCU, PECU, and IOCU can all operate in parallel.

The MPP features that contribute most to its power are its large size, the ability to perform processing and I/O simultaneously, the provisions for fault tolerance, the SUM-OR trees, the connections between the corner elements and the controller, and the staging memory. The existence of a mask register for the selective disabling of processors is also useful. The MPP processors have more memory than those in either CLIP4 or GAPP, but still more memory is needed for some algorithms.

4.5. The MasPar MP-1

The MP-1 is a commercial machine first offered by the MasPar Corporation in 1990,[159] which is based in part on the earlier Blitzen parallel computer.[30] Various sized MP-1 machines are available, the smallest of which consists of a single board with 1K processors and the largest of which comprises 16 boards and has 16K processors. Each processor has a 4-bit adder and multiplier, a barrel shifter, a 64-bit accumulator, and 40 32-bit registers. On each custom VLSI chip, 32 processors, which logically form two 4 × 4 subarrays, are integrated. These chips utilize 1.6 micron CMOS technology and have approximately 500K transistors. Each chip has 164 pins. In addition to the on-chip registers, each processor has 16K bytes of RAM located off-chip, yielding a total of 256M bytes of RAM in the largest configuration. The off-chip memory is implemented with 1M-bit dynamic RAM chips with ECC support. The clock operates with an 80-ns cycle time. The processors operate in an SIMD mode with weak uniform communication, but independent addressing is provided.

The processors are arranged in an array with each processor being connected to its eight nearest neighbors. The connections between neighboring processors, which form a communication network known as the X-net, are all 1-bit wide. The top and bottom rows and the leftmost and rightmost columns are connected, so the connections logically form a torus. In addition to the X-net connections, there is a switch-based interconnection network known as the global router. The global router does not provide connections to every PE; instead, groups of 16 PEs share each input to the router. The global router is a three-stage Omega network[145] in which each switch is a 64 × 64 crossbar. Each path in the global router is 1 bit wide. The router is circuit-switched, with circuits being bidirectional once established. Because 16 PEs share each input to the global router, because an Omega network cannot implement all permutations, and because multiple processors may attempt to access the same processor, contention in the router is likely. Communication operations that use the global router are broken into phases. When a processor is unsuccessful in establishing a connection during one phase, it waits until the next communication phase and tries again. By waiting until all processors have succeeded before initiating new communication requests, access to the network is guaranteed to all of the processors. In addition to providing global communication between processors, the global router is used for performing I/O operations at a rate of up to 1.3G bytes per second.

Although the processors operate on 4-bit quantities, the instruction set is defined in terms of 64-, 32-, 16-, and 8-bit operations. This allows the underlying hardware to evolve to an 8-bit word size without affecting any applications. Two high-level programming languages, based on C and Fortran, are provided. The language based on C allows the user to specify the placement and movement of data in the arrays, while the language based on Fortran presents a higher level abstraction in which arrays are placed automatically. The programming environment includes a symbolic debugger and animators to view the operation of programs.

The MasPar MP-1 is the newest architecture presented here, and as a result, it offers significantly more power and memory than the other mesh connected computers. The use of 4-bit, rather than 1-bit, processors and the support for independent addressing are both notable. The other unique feature of the MP-1 is its global router network. Although this network is sparse (1 connection per 16 processors), it provides rapid communication for small amounts of data over large distances.

The only disadvantage to the MP-1 appears to be low bandwidth of the nearest-neighbor connections. Although each PE is connected to its eight nearest neighbors, these connections are only 1 bit wide (while the processors are 4 bits wide). Furthermore, only one of these eight connections can be used at a time. In contrast, the much older CLIP4 provided simultaneous communication to all eight neighbors.

4.6 Three-Dimensional Mesh Connected Computers

Several recent parallel computers are based on a three-dimensional mesh or torus interconnection network. The J-machine[175] is a project at MIT consisting of up to 64K processors that are interconnected in a three-dimensional mesh topology. The routing nodes on this mesh are connected to their six neighbors by using 9-bit-wide bidirectional links transmitting data at 36 Mbyte per second. The processor used in the J-machine is custom-designed, since the so-called message-driven nature of the architecture requires a specialized processor. Other notable machines are the current efforts in Teracomputer's architecture involving up to 512 custom processors[10] and NEC's parallel processors.[269]

CHAPTER 5

Algorithms for Mesh Connected Computers

This chapter presents algorithms for solving a number of problems on mesh connected computers. The problems that were selected fall into the categories of basic communication operations, image processing, and scientific applications. The algorithms in this section will be for the *plain mesh connected computer*. A plain mesh connected computer operates in an SIMD mode. The PEs use uniform addressing in accessing their memories (all PEs access the same local memory location at any given time), and communication is weak and uniform (each PE can send a message to only one neighbor at a time, and all PEs communicate in the same direction). The PEs can be selectively disabled by using mask registers. The top and bottom rows and the leftmost and rightmost columns are connected, so that the interconnections logically form a torus. It should be noted, however, that a machine that does not have these "wraparound" connections can simulate a machine that does have them with only a constant factor increase in time. In particular, consider a $P^{1/2} \times P^{1/2}$ mesh connected computer without wraparound connections, where $P^{1/2}$ is an even integer. Let the function $f(i)$ be defined such that $f(i) = 2i$, if $0 \leq i < P^{1/2}/2$, and $f(i) = 2P^{1/2} - 2i - 1$, if $P^{1/2} \leq i < P^{1/2}$. Each processor (i, j) of a $P^{1/2} \times P^{1/2}$ mesh with wraparounds is mapped to processor $[f(i), f(j)]$ of a $P^{1/2} \times P^{1/2}$ mesh without wraparounds. It is easy to see that a single communication operation in the simulated machine (with wraparound connections) can be implemented with, at most, four communication operations on the actual machine (without wraparound connections).

The plain mesh connected computer consists of P PEs arranged in a $P^{1/2} \times P^{1/2}$ array. Each PE has a constant number of words of memory, where each word has $O(\log N)$ bits (all logarithms in this book are in base 2). Unless stated otherwise, the algorithms will be for the case $N = P$. Although it is common in practice for N to be larger than P, the algorithm for the case $N = P$ can be used when $N > P$ by simulating an N processor mesh connected computer. Specifically, each of the P real processors is assigned N/P virtual processors, which form an $(N/P)^{1/2} \times (N/P)^{1/2}$ window in the virtual machine. With this assignment of virtual processors to real processors, the P

processor machine can simulate the N processor machine with a factor of N/P slowdown.[83] In some cases, the factor of N/P slowdown can be reduced by modifying the algorithm that is used.

For the following algorithms, it is assumed that the input data are stored in the processors' local memories. For example, the image processing algorithms begin with an $N^{1/2} \times N^{1/2}$ pixel image that is stored in the local memories, one pixel per PE. Similarly, the matrix multiplication algorithm begins with two $N^{1/2} \times N^{1/2}$ matrices stored in the local memories, with the entries from the i-th row and j-th column of both matrices stored in the PE in the i-th row and j-th column.

For some algorithms, it will be assumed that the row and column coordinates of each PE are stored in the PE's RAM. This can be accomplished by using an external computer to create a $P^{1/2} \times P^{1/2}$ array of coordinates and then shifting the coordinates into the array of PEs one column at a time. Although all of the problems in this section will first be solved using a plain mesh connected computer, algorithms for some extensions to this model will also be presented. One such extension will be called the *mesh plus tree computer*. This machine consists of a plain mesh connected computer plus a binary tree of PEs that has the PEs in the mesh connected computer at the leaves of the tree. Such a machine can be used to quickly extract small amounts of information from the image.

The time analysis of the algorithms will be in terms of simple operations on one word quantities, where a word contains $O(\log N)$ bits. The time analysis will be for the worst case data.

5.1 Table Lookup Operation

Here each PE holds a single value in the range 0 through $V - 1$, and the object is to calculate, for each value i, the function $F(i)$. The function F is defined by a lookup table with V entries. A simple algorithm for this problem requires $O(V)$ time. The V values of the lookup table are broadcast to the array one at a time, with only the PEs containing the appropriate pixel value being enabled to receive the broadcast value. The reason table lookup operations are so slow is that it is impossible to access different RAM locations in different PEs in parallel. If such independent addressing was possible and if each PE had its own copy of the lookup table, a table lookup operation could be performed in one step. Of course, loading a copy of the table into each PE consumes both $O(V)$ time and memory per PE, so this approach would be worthwhile only if the table were to be used a number of times.

A faster algorithm for this problem will be given in Section 5.8. That algorithm requires only a constant amount of memory per PE and solves the problem in $O(V^{1/2})$ time, assuming that the lookup table has already been loaded in the memory of the PEs.

5.2 $M \times M$ Convolution

An $M \times M$ convolution is an image processing operation that replaces each pixel with a weighted average of the pixels in a $M \times M$ pixel window centered on that pixel. The weight of each pixel is determined by its position within the $M \times M$ window. Convolutions are used to smooth images and reduce the effects of noise. Some convolutions are separable, which means that they can be divided into two convolutions, one of which smooths along rows and the other along columns. Here, it is assumed that the convolution is inseparable, so each PE must examine all M^2 pixels in its $M \times M$ window.

An $M \times M$ convolution can be performed in $O(M^2)$ time on a plain mesh connected computer with $P = N$ processors. The key feature of the algorithm is an efficient technique for moving all pixels in each $M \times M$ window to the PE at the center of the window. If the pixels in each $M \times M$ window are accessed in an arbitrary order, the pixels near the corners of the window will require $M - 1$ shifts and the algorithm will require $O(M^3)$ time. However, by accessing the pixels in the correct order, the algorithm can be reduced to $O(M^2)$ time. First, the controller broadcasts the weight of the center pixel in the $M \times M$ window, each PE multiplies its pixel by this weight, and the result is stored in a running total variable. Then the image is shifted 1 PE to the left. At this point, the controller broadcasts the weight of the pixel just to the right of the center in the $M \times M$ window, this weight is multiplied by the pixel currently in the PE, and the result is added to the running total variable. Then the image is shifted down 1 PE. Again, the appropriate weight is broadcast from the controller, this weight is multiplied by the pixel currently in the PE, and the result is added to the running total variable. This process is repeated so that all of the pixels in each $M \times M$ window are accessed in a spiral order. The entire algorithm requires a total of $M^2 - 1$ communication operations. Details of this algorithm, and extensions of the algorithm to various shapes of windows are presented in Refs. 79 and 146.

An $M \times M$ convolution is an example of a local neighborhood operation, because each pixel is replaced by a function of itself and the pixels in a small region around it. Many other local neighborhood operations defined on $M \times M$ windows can also be performed in $O(M^2)$ time on a plain mesh connected computer. For example, a binary morphological operation, which consists of a boolean function of the $M \times M$ windows in a binary image, can be completed in this time.

5.3 Finding the Value and Location of a Global Maximum

There are a number of situations in which it is useful to find the maximum or minimum value of a data set. On a plain mesh connected computer with $P = N$ processors, the value and location of a global maximum (or minimum) can be found in $O(N^{1/2})$ time. The algorithm consists of first finding the maxima for the columns and then comparing these column maxima to obtain the global maximum. The column maxima are found by first shifting a copy of the data items down one row, along with the items' associated x and y coordinates. The unshifted and shifted items are compared and the larger item and its coordinates are stored. Next, the larger item and its coordinates are shifted down two rows and another comparison is performed. Then the data are shifted down four rows and compared again. This pattern is repeated until the column maxima have been calculated. Then the global maximum is found by performing the same set of shift and compare operations in a horizontal direction. If a data item or its coordinates can be sent to a neighboring PE in one operation, then a total of $4N^{1/2} - 4$ communication operations are required.

If a tree of OR gates is available, which gives the controller the OR of a particular 1-bit register in the PEs, and if all of the data items are in the range 0 through $V - 1$, an $O(\log V + \log N)$ time algorithm is possible. The algorithm starts by using the tree of OR gates to see whether any data items have a 1 in their most significant bit position. If any items do have such a 1, then the PEs containing items with a 0 in their most significant bit position are disabled (by setting their mask registers) for the remainder of the algorithm. The procedure is then repeated for successively less significant bit positions, until all of the $\log V$ bit positions have been processed. At this point, only PEs that contain an item that is a global maximum are enabled. The location of one of these PEs (namely the one with the highest row-major index) is transmitted to the controller by processing the bit positions of the x and y coordinates in the same manner. A similar algorithm for the MPP is given in Ref. 70.

On a mesh plus tree computer, the value and location of a maximum can be determined in $O(\log N)$ time. The algorithm is very simple. In each of the $O(\log N)$ steps, the data items and coordinates are moved one level up in the tree. Each PE at this higher level compares the items sent to it by its children and saves only the larger received item and its coordinates. At the end of this procedure, the root of the tree will contain the value and location of a global maximum.

When $N > P$, the value and location of a maximum can be found in $O(N/P + P^{1/2})$ time.[161] Each processor first examines the N/P items in its local memory and determines which is largest. Then, the P items that are the largest in their respective PEs are used as the input to the $N = P$ maximum finding algorithm. This result is surprising because when $P < N$, not only is the factor of N/P slowdown avoided, but the resulting algorithm is often faster than the $P = N$ algorithm! In particular, the fastest algorithm is obtained when $P = N^{2/3}$ at which point the algorithm requires $O(N^{1/3})$ time. This value of P balances the number of items per processor with the diameter of the mesh (the maximum number of links that must be crossed to send a message between two PEs).

5.4 Histogram

For this problem, it will be assumed that each PE contains a single data item that is in the range 0 through $V - 1$. The object is to calculate, for each value 0 through $V - 1$, the number of items that have that value. On a plain mesh connected computer, a histogram can be calculated in $O(V + N^{1/2})$ time. The algorithm for the case $V \leq N^{1/2}$ will be given first. It begins by calculating histograms for the columns in parallel, and then adding the column histograms to obtain the histogram for the entire array. The column histograms are calculated by shifting the data items down $N^{1/2}$ times (in a cyclical manner using the connections between the bottom and top rows) and adding one to a counter in each PE whenever an item's value matches the row number of the PE in which it is stored. After this procedure, the PE in position (i, j) has the number of items with value i that are in column j. At this point, the column histograms have been calculated.

The column histograms are then combined into a single histogram by first shifting the column histograms 1 PE to the left and adding them together, then shifting them 2 PEs to the left and adding them together, then shifting them 4 PEs to the left and adding, etc. After $N^{1/2} - 1$ horizontal shifts, the histogram values are in the leftmost column. The entire algorithm requires $2N^{1/2} - 1$ communication operations and a similar number of additions. The details of this algorithm can be found in Ref. 141. A variant of this algorithm that is designed for bit-serial machines appears in Ref. 49. That variant requires $O(VN^{1/2})$ bit operations, while the algorithm described here uses $O(N^{1/2} \log N)$ bit operations.

If $V > N^{1/2}$, the V possible values are divided into $O(V/N)$ sets of at most N values each. The above algorithm is used to calculate the histogram for each set of values in $O(N^{1/2})$ time, so the entire algorithm requires $O(V)$ time.

On a mesh plus tree computer, a histogram can be calculated in $O(V + \log N)$ time. This algorithm uses the tree of PEs to count the number of items with value 0, then the number of items with value 1, etc., until all V values have been counted. Because the counts for each value all occupy the same level of the tree at any one time, it is possible to pipeline the counting of successive values. A similar algorithm is given in Ref. 202, where the use of special purpose bit counting hardware is discussed.

5.5 Hough (or Radon) Transform

The Hough (or Radon) transform of an image is a set of projections of the image from different angles.[214] This transform has many uses, the most common of which is locating straight lines in an image. The Hough transform can be defined formally as follows. There is a set of Q angles, $\theta_1, \theta_2, \ldots, \theta_Q$, along which projections are taken. For each projection, the image is divided into bands that are 1 pixel wide and oriented according to the projection angle.

Each projection consists of K numbers, $b_1, b_2, \ldots, b_K$, where b_I is the sum of the gray levels of all the pixels that have their center in band number I. It is fair to assume that $0 < \theta \le \pi$, because projections are the same for θ and for $\theta + \pi$ regardless of the value of θ.

An $O(QN^{1/2})$ time Hough transform algorithm is given in Ref. 228. That algorithm calculates the projections for the Q different values of θ separately. For each value of θ, the controller first broadcasts the values $\sin(\theta)$ and $\cos(\theta)$ to all of the PEs. Each PE calculates $z = x^* \cos(\theta) + y^* \sin(\theta)$, where x and y are the row and column coordinates of the pixel in the PE. The value z is the distance from the origin to the line that passes through the point (x, y) and is at angle θ with respect to the y axis. Next, each PE calculates $w = $ floor(z), which is the distance from the origin to the 1-pixel-wide band that passes through (x, y) at the desired angle. Each PE then creates a record containing its pixel value and the variable w. These records are totaled by using an algorithm that is similar to the plain mesh connected computer histogram algorithm presented in Section 5.4. Specifically, the records are shifted down $N^{1/2}$ times (cyclically, using the connections between the top and bottom rows). After each of these shifts, those PEs that are holding a record with a w field that matches the PE's row number increase a running total variable by the pixel field of the record. After these $N^{1/2}$ shifts and adds, the PE in position (i, j) has the contribution of the pixels in column j to band i for the current value of θ. Then, the running total variables within each row are summed together. At this point, the projection for the current value of θ has been calculated. This entire procedure is repeated for each of the Q values of θ.

A number of more efficient Hough transform algorithms appear in Refs. 60 and 97. Both papers contain similar $O(Q + N^{1/2})$ time algorithms. The $O(Q + N^{1/2})$ time algorithm from Ref. 60 will be described here. The algorithm calculates the value of a single band for a single value of θ by sweeping a variable (called band_total) over the image. Each band_total follows its band across the image. As a band_total passes over a pixel in its band, it adds the pixel's value to itself.

The projection angles are first divided into two groups. The first group contains angles where $(\pi/4) < \theta \le 3(\pi/4)$, and the second group contains angles where $0 < \theta \le (\pi/4)$ or $3(\pi/4) < \theta \le \pi$. The groups are processed separately. The processing of the projections in the first group, which have bands that are more horizontal than vertical, will be examined first. Because the bands are only 1 pixel wide and are more horizontal than vertical, each band contains at most 2 pixels in each column. One approach would be to have each band_total visit all of the PEs that have pixels in its band. However, this is inefficient because some band_totals would have to visit 2 PEs in some columns. Instead, two versions of the image are used: the original image and a copy of the image shifted vertically 1 position. Each band_total can now visit the 1 or 2 pixels in its band in a given column by visiting just a single PE.

The algorithm begins by placing the band_totals for the first projection angle, initialized to 0, in the first column of PEs. Each band_total is placed so that it lies above the pixel or pixels in its band. The band_totals are increased by the values of the pixels that lie beneath them. Then, they are shifted from the first to the second column. Next, a vertical shift is performed so that each band_total once again lies above the pixel or pixels in its band. Now, the band_totals for the next projection angle are initialized to 0 and placed in the first column. The band_totals for both projections increase themselves by the values of the pixels beneath them. Then, both columns of band_totals are shifted one column to the right and the band_totals for the next projection are started in the first column. This process is repeated until all of the projections in the first group have been calculated. Then the second group is processed in a similar manner, with the roles of rows and columns reversed.

In addition to moving the band_totals across the image, the values $\sin(\theta)$ and $\cos(\theta)$ must also be be shifted across the image so that the band_totals can follow paths that keep them above pixels in their correct bands. This increases the amount of communication that is required, thus, slowing the algorithm. In particular, the algorithm as specified in Ref. 60 requires $20Q + 48N^{1/2} + 4$ communication operations, and a similar number of local operations, to calculate the Hough transform. While this is fairly fast, it is possible to improve the speed in certain situations. If the same set of projection angles is used for calculating the Hough transform for a large number of images, the values of $\sin(\theta)$ and $\cos(\theta)$ do not have to be shifted across the image. This is because the the path of each band_total variable across the image is completely determined by the values of θ chosen for the Hough transform. Instead of shifting the values of $\sin(\theta)$ and $\cos(\theta)$ across the image to calculate the paths of the band_totals, the paths can be precomputed and stored in the PEs. When this approach is used, only $6Q + 14N^{1/2} + 4$ communication operations are required.

5.6 Dense Matrix Multiplication

The problem of multiplying two matrices is fundamental not only to many scientific applications, but also to several graph theoretical applications. For example, the all-pairs shortest distance problem, the transitive closure, and topological sorting can all be solved with matrix multiplication.[69] A very simple $O(N^{1/2})$ time matrix multiplication algorithm for mesh connected computers that was created by Cannon[36,69] will be described.

Let $\mathbf{A}$ and $\mathbf{B}$ be the matrices to be multiplied, and let $\mathbf{C}$ be the resultant matrix. Each entry $c_{i,j}$ in $\mathbf{C}$ is the sum, over all values of k from 1 through $N^{1/2}$, of $a_{i,k} * b_{k,j}$. In other words, to calculate $c_{i,j}$ the entries in row i of $\mathbf{A}$ must be multiplied by the corresponding entries in column j of $\mathbf{B}$. Cannon's algorithm has two phases. In the first phase, the matrices $\mathbf{A}$ and $\mathbf{B}$ are shifted so that corresponding entries are located in the same PE. Then, in the second phase, each entry $c_{i,j}$ in **C** is calculated by successively shifting **A** and **B** so that all of the pairs $a_{i,k}$ and $b_{k,j}$ visit PE (i,j).

Specifically, the first phase circularly shifts each row i of **A** to the left i times and each column j of **B** upwards j times. At this point, each PE (i,j) holds $a_{i,k}$ and $b_{k,j}$, where $k = i + j \bmod N^{1/2}$, so corresponding entries are stored in the same PE.

The second phase then multiplies the pairs $a_{i,k}$ and $b_{k,j}$ and the result is stored in a running total variable. Then, the entries in **A** are circularly shifted left one position and the entries in **B** are circularly shifted up one position. At this point, each PE (i,j) holds $a_{i,k}$ and $b_{k,j}$, where $k = i + j + 1 \bmod N^{1/2}$. The process of multiplying the pairs $a_{i,k}$ and $b_{k,j}$ and then shifting the **A** and **B** matrices is repeated a total of $N^{1/2}$ times to obtain the desired result. The entire algorithm requires a total of $4N^{1/2} - 4$ communication steps (the savings of 4 comes from numbering the rows and columns from 0 in the first phase and from eliminating the final shifts in the second phase).

5.7 Sorting

To define the sorting problem for plain mesh connected computers, an indexing function that assigns each number in the range 0 through $N - 1$ to a unique PE must be defined. The object is to reorder the data items so that the k-th largest item is stored in the PE with index k. The three most common indexing schemes are the row-major, the shuffled row-major, and the snakelike row-major.[248] Let $n = N^{1/2}$. It is assumed that the PEs are initially labeled with pairs of the form (i,j), $0 \le iN^{1/2}$, $0 \le jN^{1/2}$. In the row-major indexing scheme, PE (i,j) is assigned index $iN^{1/2} + j$. An equivalent definition of row-major indexing is that the PE in row i and column j is assigned the index with binary representation $(i_{(n-1)}, i_{(n-2)}, \ldots, i_{(0)}, j_{(n-1)}, j_{(n-2)}, \ldots, j_{(0)})$. In shuffled row-major indexing, the PE in row i and column j is assigned the index with binary representation $(i_{(n-1)}, j_{(n-1)}, i_{(n-2)}, j_{(n-2)}, \ldots, i_{(0)}, j_{(0)})$. The snakelike row-major indexing is obtained from the row-major indexing by reversing the order of every other row, so that the first row increases from left to right, the next row increases from right to left, etc. While the row-major indexing scheme might seem the most natural, it turns out that the other indexing schemes match the structure of certain sorting algorithms.

Quite a few $O(N^{1/2})$ time algorithms have been devised for sorting N items on a mesh connected computer with $P = N$ processors.[138,144,158,168,209,215,217,218,248] These algorithms have different constants of proportionality in their running times, they use different indexing functions, and they run on slightly different models of mesh connected computers.

The first $O(N^{1/2})$ time algorithms were shown by Thompson and Kung.[248] They demonstrated that Batcher's bitonic sort[16] can be used to obtain a shuffled row-major ordering of the data with $14(N^{1/2} - 1) - 4 \log N$ communication steps. In fact, their algorithm runs on a plain mesh connected computer without wraparound connections, and approximately $(3/2)N^{1/2}$ communication steps can be eliminated if wraparound connections are present.

Thompson and Kung's algorithm is particularly interesting because it can be viewed as being a simulation of the hypercube bitonic sorting algorithm, which will be discussed in Section 10.7.1. The bitonic sorting algorithm is composed of $O(\log^2 N)$ compare-exchange stages. In each compare-exchange stage, the N items are divided into $N/2$ pairs of items, the items in each pair are compared, and they are swapped if they are not in the desired order. When the bitonic sort is implemented on a hypercube computer, all of the comparisons are between items in PEs that are connected by a communications link, so the entire algorithm runs in $O(\log^2 N)$ time. When the bitonic sort is run on a mesh connected computer, the pairs of items that must be compared are often far apart. As a result, a series of shifts have to be performed to bring the pairs of items together. Interestingly enough, when the shuffled row-major indexing is used and the mesh processor with index k simulates hypercube processor number k, an asymptotically optimal sorting algorithm is obtained. It is also interesting to note that when the same approach is used with the row-major indexing, an $O(N^{1/2} \log N)$ time algorithm is obtained.[179] Finally, it should be mentioned that Nassimi and Sahni developed a technique based on the bitonic sort, which obtains a row-major ordering of the data in $O(N^{1/2})$ time. Nassimi and Sahni's algorithm is different in that it cannot be viewed as being a direct simulation of the hypercube algorithm.

Several other sorting algorithms have been created that have smaller constants of proportionality than Thompson and Kung's bitonic sort. Specifically, the algorithms developed by Schnorr and Shamir[218] and by Ma, Sen, and Scherson[158] have very small constants of proportionality associated with the $N^{1/2}$ term. However, they have very large smaller order terms that make them impractical for realistic values of N. Two practical sorting algorithms for mesh connected computers were given by Sado and Igarashi.[209] Their algorithms consist entirely of compare-exchange stages in which the pairs of items that are being compared are neighbors in the mesh. Their first algorithm requires $(6.5)N^{1/2} + \log N - 5$ compare-exchange stages, while their second one requires $(5.75)N^{1/2} + 5 \log N - 49$ compare-exchange stages if $N \geq 256$. Each compare-exchange stage requires two communication operations on a plain mesh connected computer, so their algorithms are only slightly faster than Thompson and Kung's bitonic sort. However, if a mesh connected computer with weak independent communication is used, and if data can be sent in both directions across a link simultaneously, each compare-exchange stage requires just one communication operation and Sado and Igarashi's algorithms are significantly faster. Both of their algorithms can yield either a row-major or a snakelike row-major ordering in the given time bounds, and neither algorithm requires wraparound connections.

Another interesting sorting algorithm for mesh connected computers is the shear-sort algorithm created by Scherson, Sen, and Shamir.[216] Although shear-sort requires a suboptimal $O(N^{1/2} \log N)$ time, it has particularly simple control and is easy to describe. Shear-sort consists of ceiling $((\log N)/2) + 1$ phases, each of which is composed of a "row sort" followed by a "column sort." Each row sort consists of sorting within the rows, with even-numbered rows being sorted in ascending order and odd-numbered rows being sorted in descending order. Each column sort consists of sorting within the columns, every column being sorted in ascending order. At the completion of the algorithm, the items are arranged in a snakelike row-major order.

The row sorts and column sorts can be implemented with simple parallel versions of bubble-sort.[132, 209] Specifically, a linear array of $N^{1/2}$ items can be sorted with $N^{1/2}$ compare-exchange stages. In each of the even- (odd-) numbered compare-exchange stages, each item in an even-numbered position in the array is compared with the item following (preceding) it, and they are exchanged if they are out of order.

5.8 Pointer-Based Communication

There are many situations in which it is useful to perform communication in a data-dependent manner. Two very important routines for performing data-dependent communication are the random access write (RAW) and the random access read (RAR). These routines allow PEs to communicate according to a pattern that is represented by pointer variables located in the PEs. As a result, they allow the programmer to view the mesh connected computer as a shared memory machine. The RAW and RAR routines are very important in symbolic processing, which often involves lists, graphs, and other pointer-based data structures.

The RAW and RAR routines are defined formally as follows. For both routines, each PE begins with a piece of data in its S (source) register and a pointer to another PE in its Q register. In a RAW, each PE transfers the contents of its S register to the PE specified by its Q register. The transferred data are stored in the PEs' D (destination) registers. Conflicts arising from two PEs sending data to the same PE can be resolved in a number of ways. For example, the minimum or the sum of the values received by a PE could be stored. In a RAR, each PE receives the contents of the S register of the PE specified by its Q register. The received values are stored in the D registers. Note that multiple PEs may read the data from a single PE in a RAR operation.

In Ref. 166, $O(N^{1/2})$ time RAW and RAR algorithms for plain mesh connected computers are presented. The RAW algorithm presented in that paper can be divided into two parts. In the first part of the algorithm, each PE creates a record with its Q and S values, and these records are sorted according to their Q values. The sorting is accomplished by using a bitonic sort,[16,168], but any of the sorting algorithms described above could be used. The second part of the algorithm consists of handling conflicts that arise from having more than one record with the same Q field and then delivering the records to their final destinations. The RAR algorithm is similar to the RAW algorithm, except that it consists of a request phase in which requests for data are sent and a delivery phase in which the requests are satisfied. As was the case with Thompson and Kung's implementation of the bitonic sorting algorithm discussed above, Nassimi and Sahni's RAW and RAR algorithms can be viewed as direct simulations of hypercube algorithms.

Although both the RAW and RAR algorithms presented in Ref. 166 require only $O(N^{1/2})$ time, the constants of proportionality in the time analysis are quite large. In particular, if the D and Q registers are each one word long and if a word can be sent between neighboring PEs in one step, the RAW algorithm requires over $50N^{1/2}$ communication operations and the RAR algorithm requires over $100N^{1/2}$ communication operations. However, if each PE has $O(N^{1/2})$ words of memory and if the PEs have the ability to perform independent addressing, much faster $O(N^{1/2})$ time RAW and RAR algorithms are possible. Two such algorithms will be presented next. They are simple generalizations of a natural greedy algorithm that is well-known for routing permutations. The RAW algorithm presented here requires $4N^{1/2}$ communication operations, and the RAR algorithm presented here requires $5N^{1/2}$ communication operations.

To simplify the presentation, it will first be assumed that no two PEs attempt to write to the same PE. First, each PE creates a record (which will be called a source record) with the contents of its S and Q registers. These records are shifted to the right $N^{1/2}$ times (cyclically, using the connections between the leftmost and rightmost columns). After each of the $N^{1/2}$ shifts, each record's Q field is checked. If the Q field points to PE (i, j) and the record is currently in column j, it is stored in location $M(i)$. Second, each PE creates a record (which will be called a destination record) consisting of its row number and its D register (which is initialized to infinity). These destination records are then cyclically shifted upwards $N^{1/2}$ times. After each shift, the row field of the record is used to index into the M array. If R is the value of the row field, and if $M(R)$ contains a source record, then the destination record's D field is set to the source record's S field. After $N^{1/2}$ vertical shifts, the RAW is completed. If it is possible that more than one PE is writing data to the same PE, the above RAW algorithm can easily be modified so that no S value is written over a smaller S value.

A simple RAR algorithm can be created using a similar technique. To perform a RAR, each PE creates a source record containing its row number and its S register. These source records are cyclically shifted upwards $N^{1/2}$ times. After each shift, the contents of the source record's S field is stored in the PE's memory at the location specified by the record's row field. Then each PE creates a destination record that contains the PE's column number, its Q register, and its D register (initialized to infinity). These destination records are cyclically shifted to the right $N^{1/2}$ times. After each shift, if the destination record's Q field points to PE (i, j) and the record is in column j, then the contents of the PE's memory location i is copied into the D field of the record. After these horizontal shifts, each PE copies the D field of the record that it holds into its D register, completing the RAR.

It was mentioned above that Nassimi and Sahni's RAW and RAR algorithms can be used to perform table lookup operations using a plain mesh connected computer. A table lookup operation can be performed in $O(V^{1/2})$ time, assuming that the lookup table has been loaded into the PEs. Because each PE has only a constant number of words of memory, it is impossible to load a copy of the entire lookup table in each PE. Instead, it will be assumed that the array of PEs is partitioned into $V^{1/2} \times V^{1/2}$ squares, with the i-th entry of the lookup table being stored in the i-th PE within each square. Given this storage of the lookup table, the lookup operation can be performed by executing a RAR within each $V^{1/2} \times V^{1/2}$ square. The data value is used as the Q variable and the lookup table entry is used as the S variable when performing the RAR. Although this algorithm has a good asymptotic complexity, the constants of proportionality are large so that the algorithm is only practical for very large V.

If there are guaranteed to be no simultaneous read or write requests to a single PE, then improved running times can be obtained. In particular, the RAW operation consists of a partial permutation and the RAR operation can be implemented by using two partial permutations (the permutation is partial if not all of the PEs participate). Leighton, Makedon, and Tollis have shown that any partial permutation can be implemented on a mesh connected computer, without wraparounds, which has strong communication and constant memory per PE in $2N^{1/2} - 2$ communication steps.[150] This result is optimal for the given type of mesh because PEs at opposite corners may have to communicate. However, this algorithm does not appear to be practical for two reasons. First, the processing needed between communication steps can be considerable, since priority queues are required within the PEs. Second, while the memory requirements per PE are constant, the creators of the algorithm have stated that the amount of memory is quite large for practical values of N.[150]

5.9 Labeling Image Connected Components

The problem of labeling image-connected components consists of giving labels (numbers) to the pixels with value 1 in a binary image, such that any two pixels have the same label if and only if they lie in the same connected component. A connected component is a maximal region of pixels with value 1, such that any two pixels in the region are the endpoints of a path that is connected and only passes through pixels with value 1. There are two common definitions of connectedness that can be used with the above definition, namely 4-connectedness and 8-connectedness. Two pixels are 4-connected if they are adjacent vertically or horizontally, and they are 8-connected if they are adjacent vertically, horizontally, or diagonally. The definition that is chosen does not seem to have an important effect on the design of the algorithm. The labeling of image-connected components is important in many applications. It allows regions (the connected components) to be identified so that the analysis of the image can be performed on a higher level than the pixel level. Different features of the regions can be calculated and used to classify or identify them.

There are a number of algorithms for labeling image-connected components on a mesh connected computer. The algorithms can be divided into two main categories: (1) local neighborhood algorithms and (2) divide-and-conquer algorithms. The local neighborhood algorithms are based on repetitively performing a neighborhood operation on all pixels in the image, while the divide-and-conquer algorithms perform component labeling on successively larger regions of the image.

One local neighborhood algorithm, which will be called the component broadcasting algorithm, is very simple. Each PE that contains a pixel with value 1 is initially given a label that is the concatenation of its x and y coordinates. Then, a series of broadcasting operations is performed. Each broadcasting operation consists of a transfer of labels from each PE with a pixel with value 1 to each of its (4-connected or 8-connected) neighbor PEs that also has a pixel with value 1. Then, each PE calculates the minimum of its current label and the labels that it has received and uses this minimum as its new label. An algorithm similar to this one is presented in Ref. 206. The time complexity of the component broadcasting algorithm is dependent on the sizes and shapes of the connected components. In an image that consists of small, convex-connected components, the algorithm provides the desired labeling very quickly. There are some possible images, however, that have very long and thin connected components that would require $O(N)$ time to label using this algorithm. One such example is shown in Figure 5.1. Thus, it is necessary either to perform the broadcasting operation a data-dependent number of times, which requires special hardware, such as the tree of OR gates discussed in Section 4.1, or to perform the broadcasting operation $O(N)$ times on all images.

Two faster local neighborhood algorithms are presented in Ref. 61. Both algorithms are based on the use of a binary morphological operation defined by S. Levialdi.[152] The value of pixel $Q(i, j)$ is determined from the previous values of the pixels $Q(i, j)$, $Q(i + 1, j)$, $Q(i, j - 1)$, and $Q(i + 1, j - 1)$. Thus, each pixel's value is determined by a 2×2 neighborhood of the pixel. The new value of pixel $Q(i, j)$ is defined to be $h\{h[Q(i, j - 1) + Q(i, j) + Q(i + 1, j) - 1] + h[Q(i, j) + Q(i + 1, j - 1) - 1]\}$, where $h(t) = 0$ for $t \leq 0$, $h(t) = 1$ for $t > 0$. The effect of this operation, which will be called the shrinking operation, can be easily understood as follows. Assume that pixel $Q(i, j)$ is in row i and column j and that pixel $Q(0, 0)$ is in the lower left-hand corner

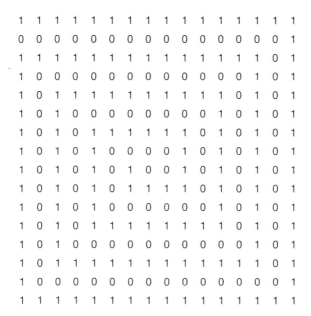

Fig. 5.1. Snakelike image.

of the image. Then, if pixel $Q(i, j)$ originally has a value of 1, it will have a value of 1 after the shrinking operation if and only if at least one of its three neighbors to the right, below, or diagonally right and below has a 1. If pixel $Q(i, j)$ originally has a value of 0, it will have a value of 1 after the shrinking operation if and only if both its neighbor to the right and its neighbor below have 1s. Levialdi has proven that when this shrinking operation is applied in parallel to all pixels in an image, only 1s that do not disconnect an object will be erased, and that 0s do not become 1s when this would connect previously unconnected regions. The shrinking operation has the effect of squeezing each connected component into the upper left-hand corner of its bounding box until only 1 pixel remains, which is then deleted by the next shrinking operation. The number of shrinking operations required to shrink an object until it contains only 1 pixel is, at most, the distance from the upper left-hand corner of the object's bounding box to the most distant pixel in the object, where the distance between the points is measured using the chessboard metric. The distance from $(x1, y1)$ to $(x2, y2)$ using the chessboard metric is defined to be $|x1 - x2| + |y1 + y2|$. As a result, every connected component will have disappeared after $2N^{1/2}$ shrinking operations.

Levialdi uses the shrinking operation to count the number of connected components. In his algorithm, whenever a connected component disappears, a special marker is created, which then moves to the lower right-hand corner of the array. Whenever two special markers arrive at the same location, a new marker that represents the sum of the previous markers is created. The marker that arrives at the lower right-hand corner after $2N^{1/2}$ iterations represents the number of connected components in the image.

The first algorithm presented in Ref. 61 requires $O(N^{1/2})$ bits of memory per PE, as opposed to the $O(\log N)$ bits per PE that are present in a plain mesh connected computer. That algorithm, which will be called the component shrinking algorithm, has two phases. In the first phase, Levialdi's shrinking operation is applied in parallel to the entire image $2N^{1/2}$ times. After each shrinking operation, a different image is obtained. The result of applying the shrinking operation y times to the original image will be called partial result y. Assume that partial result y is stored in memory location y in the PEs. In the second phase, the labels are assigned by examining the partial results in reverse order, starting with the empty image that resulted from the final shrinking operation. Stage y of the second phase, where y goes from $2N^{1/2} - 1$ to 0, consists of first transferring labels to PE (i, j) from those PEs (i, j), $(i - 1, j)$, $(i, j + 1)$, and $(i - 1, j + 1)$, that have a 1 in memory location $y + 1$. Next, any PE (i, j) that has a 1 in memory location y and that has not received a label generates a new label that is the concatenation of the numbers i, j, and y. After processing all values of y from $2N^{1/2} - 1$ to 0, each connected component will have a unique label. This can be seen by noting that a new label is created exactly for those pixels that became isolated 1s during the shrinking process. Because every component is shrunk to an isolated 1 that exists for only one stage, there is a unique label created for every connected component. The label for a component is transferred from stage y to stage $y - 1$ in a way that ensures that the label is sent to all pixels at stage $y - 1$ that correspond to the same component at stage y and to no others.

A limitation of the component shrinking algorithm is that is requires $O(N^{1/2})$ bits of memory per PE, while the component broadcasting algorithm requires only $O(\log N)$ bits of memory per PE. However, the component shrinking algorithm can be modified so that it, too, requires only $O(\log N)$ bits of memory per PE. The resulting algorithm, which will be called the log component shrinking algorithm, requires $O(N^{1/2} \log N)$ time in the worst case. That algorithm is presented in Ref. 61 and will not be repeated here.

In Ref. 169, Nassimi and Sahni present an $O(N^{1/2})$ time-connected component labeling algorithm for a plain mesh connected computer. Their algorithm operates on symbolic data structures, such as trees, so it will be referred to as the symbolic labeling algorithm. Because these trees are represented with pointers, the symbolic labeling algorithm uses the RAW and RAR routines discussed in Section 5.8. As a result, the constants of proportionality in the time complexity are very large.

The symbolic labeling algorithm uses a divide-and-conquer strategy. The algorithm has $\log N$ stages. At the beginning of the i-th stage, the image is viewed as being partitioned into square or rectangular windows, each of which contain 2^i pixels. The connected components within each of these size 2^i windows have been labeled during the previous stages. The i-th stage consists of merging pairs of adjacent labeled size 2^i windows to obtain labeled size 2^{i+1} windows. The key observation that Nassimi and Sahni make is that the size 2^{i+1} windows are already correctly labeled, except for possible inconsistencies along the border where the size 2^i windows touch. This observation is important because there are only $O(2^{i/2})$ such border pixels. As a result, these relatively few border pixels can be moved to a small square of PEs where communication operations can be performed efficiently.

It is important to remember that the above time analyses are all in terms of operations on words with $O(\log N)$ bits. However, both the component shrinking algorithm and the log component shrinking algorithm perform many of their operations on single bits. Although a machine with an $O(\log N)$ word size cannot perform bit operations any faster than it can perform full word operations, many of the actual mesh array machines use bit-serial processors. It is, therefore, interesting to analyze the complexity of the previous algorithms in terms of single-bit operations. While these algorithms can be performed on a bit-serial machine by increasing the time complexity by an $O(\log N)$ factor, the log component shrinking algorithm does not increase by this factor because many of its operations are on bits. Specifically, the component broadcasting algorithm requires $O(N \log N)$ bit operations, the component shrinking algorithm requires $O(N^{1/2} \log N)$ bit operations, the log component shrinking algorithm requires $O(N^{1/2} \log N)$ bit operations, and the symbolic labeling algorithm requires $O(N^{1/2} \log N)$ bit operations. In terms of bit operations, the log component shrinking algorithm is asymptotically as fast as the symbolic component labeling algorithm, both of which require $O(\log N)$ bits of memory per PE. However, when the constants of proportionality in the time analyses are considered, the log component shrinking algorithm is much faster. In particular, the log component shrinking algorithm requires approximately $7N^{1/2} \log N$ bit communication operations, and the symbolic labeling algorithm requires over $500N^{1/2} \log N$ bit communication operations to label 4-connected components.

When $P < N$, Miller and Stout have shown that the connected components of an image can be labeled in $O(N/P + P^{1/2})$ time.[161] Their algorithm assigns a square window of N/P pixels to each PE. The PEs first label the connected components within their windows. Then the borders of the different windows are made compatible over successively larger areas by using the symbolic labeling algorithm created by Nassimi and Sahni.[169] As was the case with the maximum finding algorithm discussed above, the asymptotically fastest algorithm is obtained when $P = N^{2/3}$, at which point an $O(N^{1/3})$ time algorithm is obtained. However, because the symbolic labeling algorithm is used when $P < N$, the constants of proportionality are increased. As a result, the fastest algorithm in practice is probably obtained when $P = N$.

5.10 Conclusions for Mesh Connected Computers

This chapter has examined a number of algorithms for mesh connected computers. The problems studied in this section can be divided in two groups. The first group contains problems that can be solved on a plain mesh connected computer in an amount of time that is independent of P, the size of the computer. This group consists of the table lookup operation and the local neighborhood operations. The second group contains problems that can be solved on a plain mesh connected computer in time that is proportional to $P^{1/2}$, the length of one side of the array. This group includes all of the remaining problems studied, including maximum location, histogram and Hough transform calculation, dense matrix multiplication, sorting, pointer-based communication, and image-connected component labeling. The plain mesh connected computer is sometimes criticized because its I/O operations require $O(N^{1/2})$ time. However, it is clear that I/O operations will not contribute greatly to the total processing time unless the only problems that are solved belong to the first group mentioned above.

A number of the problems in the second group require $O(N^{1/2})$ communication operations but perform only $O(\log N)$ calculations. As a result, some of these problems can be solved more quickly when the plain mesh connected computer is augmented with a tree of processors. For example, both the maximum location and histogram calculation problems can be solved more quickly when a tree of processors is added. Besides augmenting the plain mesh connected computer with a tree of processors, a number of other modifications to the plain mesh connected computer have been proposed. A number of authors have considered the advantages of adding a single global bus[31] or adding multiple buses.[2,194,234] The buses can be used to reduce the number of communication operations when a small amount of data must be moved a large distance. Other authors have examined the use of bypass circuitry to speed such communication.[130,153]

The greatest strengths of the mesh connected computer are its ease of construction and its performance on local neighborhood operations. Its greatest weakness is the fact that it has an $O(N^{1/2})$ diameter and, thus, requires $O(N^{1/2})$ time to solve problems involving global communication. The pointer-based communication operations discussed in Section 5.8 are particularly slow on the plain mesh connected computer. As a result, the plain mesh connected computer seems very poorly suited to performing symbolic processing. However, it was shown that the addition of $O(N^{1/2})$ words of memory per PE and the ability to perform indirect addressing provided a substantial improvement in performing pointer-based communication.

Finally, several machines and algorithms have been examined in detail. A number of other machines and algorithms have been discussed in the literature. Some of these other results can be found in Refs. 77, 93, 112, 177, and 235.

CHAPTER 6

Pyramid Machines

6.1 Introduction to Pyramids

An architecture that is related to the mesh connected computer is the pyramid. Pyramid computers have been studied for a variety of applications, but the primary motivation for the pyramid topology is the solution of image processing tasks. While there are a number of variations, a typical version is described here (see Figure 6.1). A pyramid machine consists of $(1/2)\log P + 1$ levels, where the i-th level, $0 \leq i \leq (1/2)\log P$, is a mesh connected computer with $P/2^i$ PEs. Each level has connections to the levels above and below, giving each internal PE nine connections: four to its children in the level below, four to its nearest neighbors at the same level, and one to its parent in the level above. All of the PEs operate in an SIMD mode under the direction of a single controller. The local memory accesses use uniform addressing, and communication between processors uses the weak uniform communication model.

A pyramid computer is very similar to a mesh plus tree computer. The main difference is that the pyramid computer has horizontal connections at each level, while a mesh plus tree computer has horizontal connections only at the lowest level. It is more difficult to layout a pyramid in two dimensions than it is to layout a mesh connected computer. Possibly as a result of this difficulty, no large pyramid machines have been built. However, a number of small pyramids have been built, and a number of large pyramids are currently under construction. The remainder of this section will consist of a brief examination of these machines, an analysis of a number of algorithms on pyramids, and some conclusions.

6.2 The HCL Pyramid

A prototype pyramid machine has been created at the University of Washington under the direction of S. Tanimoto.[244] The pyramid machine is designed to implement a particular set of operations known as **hierarchical**

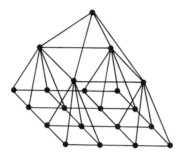

Fig. 6.1. Typical pyramid interconnection.

cellular logic (HCL),[243] therefore, the machine will be referred to as the HCL pyramid. The HCL pyramid consists of 4 levels, containing 64, 16, 4, and 1 bit-serial PEs, respectively. Each PE is viewed as being connected to 13 other PEs: 1 parent, 8 neighbors at its own level, and 4 children. Thus, each PE has an immediate neighborhood of 14 PEs (its 13 neighbors and itself). As will be discussed shortly, the actual hardware implementation has a somewhat different interconnection structure. The HCL pyramid consists of custom 64-pin NMOS chips, each of which contains a 4 × 4 array of PEs from a single level of the pyramid. Each PE contains three internal 1-bit registers, called C, L, and P, and has access to 8K bits of memory located off-chip. The HCL pyramid uses uniform addressing, but some autonomy between processors is obtained by using the C register as a mask register.

The HCL pyramid has only six instructions: *AND_Match, OR_Match, store, load, clear,* and *set.* The store instruction copies an internal register to an off-chip memory location, and the load instruction copies data in the opposite direction. The clear instruction sets an internal register to 0, while the set instruction sets an internal register to 1.

The actual processing is performed by using the AND_Match and OR_Match instructions. These instructions are the basis of what Tanimoto refers to as HCL. Both the AND_match and OR_match instructions perform a pattern matching operation on the immediate neighborhood of each PE in the pyramid. For both of these instructions, each PE calculates a single bit based on the values of a given register in its immediate neighborhood and the value of the PE's own L register. Both instructions include a 15-element pattern, where each element is 0, 1, or *D.* In the AND_Match operation, the 15 bits from each PE's immediate neighborhood are compared to the 15 pattern elements, and the results of these 15 comparisons are ANDed together. A 0 pattern element returns TRUE if the corresponding pyramid bit is a 0, a 1 pattern element returns TRUE if the corresponding pyramid bit is a 1, and a *D* pattern element always returns TRUE. The OR_Match operation is identical, except that a *D* pattern element always returns FALSE and the results of the 15 comparisons are ORed together.

As was mentioned above, the actual hardware does not have direct connections between each PE and its 13 immediate neighbors. Including all of these connections would require a total of 64 connections from the PEs on a single chip to their child PEs, which would cause a shortage of pins. The solution to this problem comes from the fact that all communication takes place as a result of AND_Match and OR_Match operations. As a result, part of each AND_Match or OR_Match can be performed on the chip containing the child PEs, and only a single bit is required from each set of four child PEs. In addition to the connections already mentioned, the HCL pyramid also has a tree of OR gates for terminating operations in a data-dependent manner. I/O is performed sequentially by a host computer that can write and read the external memory of the PEs in the base of the pyramid.

The strongest features of the HCL pyramid are its relatively large amount of memory per PE (8K bits) and its ability to perform neighborhood operations quickly. The greatest weakness of the HCL pyramid is the fact that it lacks the computational abilities of a full adder. As a result, it seems likely that arithmetic operations would be particularly slow. Also, the sequential I/O operations would be a serious bottleneck in a larger pyramid machine.

6.3 The MPP Pyramid

The MPP pyramid was built at George Mason University under the direction of D. Shaefer.[224] It is composed of MPP chips (see Section 4.4) that have been arranged in a pyramid. The MPP pyramid has five levels, with a 16 × 16 array at the base. Each PE is connected to nine other PEs: one parent, four neighbors in the same level, and four children. The pyramidal connections are implemented by multiplexing the pins. The design of the chips is discussed in Section 4.4.

6.4 The SPHINX

The SPHINX pyramid is being built at the Paris-Sud University.[160] Each layer has one-half, as opposed to the more common one-fourth, as many PEs as the layer immediately below. The levels alternate between reducing the size of the x and y dimensions of the array. Each PE is connected to its four nearest neighbors in the same level, so each internal PE has seven direct connections to other PEs. The layout of a single SPHINX PE is shown in Figure 6.2. The PEs have bit-serial processors that are capable of performing all of the 16 boolean functions of 2 inputs, as well as a number of arithmetic operations. Each PE has 64 bits of memory and a number of registers, one of which is used as a mask register. The PEs within each level are connected by a tree of OR gates that can be used to terminate repetitive operations in a

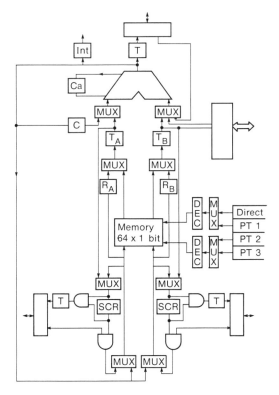

Fig. 6.2. SPHINX processor layout [© 1985 IEEE].

data-dependent manner. A separate controller is provided for each level of the pyramid, thus, allowing **m**ultiple SIMD (MSIMD) operation. Memory locations are specified by three internal pointers that are incremented or decremented by certain instructions. Presumably, this arrangement permits some degree of independence in addressing.

6.5 PAPIA

A number of Italian universities and companies are engaged in an ambitious project to create a pyramid machine, called PAPIA, that will contain 21,845 PEs.[38] The lowest level will contain 16K PEs arranged in a 128 × 128 array, with each remaining level containing one-fourth as many PEs as the level below. The entire pyramid has eight levels, each of which has a separate controller, so MSIMD operation is possible. Each internal PE is connected to its four nearest neighbors in the same level, and therefore, has a total of nine direct connections to other PEs. Either the four connected PEs in the same level or the five connected PEs in the adjacent levels can be accessed in

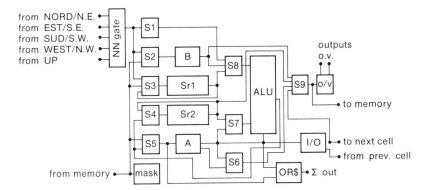

Fig. 6.3. PAPIA processor design [Cantoni, 1985].

parallel. A tree of OR gates connects the PEs in each level. I/O is performed by shifting the image in or out of the lowest level one column at a time. I/O operations can be overlapped with data processing.

The layout of a single PAPIA PE is shown in Figure 6.3. Each PE in PAPIA contains a bit-serial processor, two 1-bit registers called A and B, two 32-bit shift registers called Sr1 and Sr2, and 256 bits of RAM located on chip. The A and B registers can be used as inputs to the processor for performing boolean operations. Bit-serial arithmetic operations take inputs from the shift registers and place the results in one of them (Sr2). The logical length of the shift registers can be set by the programmer. The processor is capable of performing boolean operations with 2 inputs as well as performing a full add of 2 inputs and an internal carry register.

PAPIA is built from custom chips, each of which contains five PEs. The chips use 4 micron Si-gate NMOS technology. Each chip is 5×5 mm in size and has 48 pins. It is expected that a 200-ns clock cycle can be used. The five PEs in a chip form a small, two-level pyramid. Because 17 chips are placed on a board, each board has a four-level pyramid of PEs. The entire machine consists of 257 such boards arranged as a 16×16 array of boards topped with a single board.

The primary strengths of the PAPIA are its large size and its ability to perform arithmetic operations quickly. The existence of a full adder and of a local shift register should permit fast additions and multiplications. The primary weakness is its relatively small amount of memory per PE (256 bits).

CHAPTER 7

Algorithms for Pyramid Machines

This chapter analyzes pyramid algorithms for solving the problems considered in Chapter 5. All problems will be solved on a pyramid computer having a $P^{1/2} \times P^{1/2}$ base. Each level of the pyramid contains one-fourth as many PEs as the next lower level. All algorithms operate on N data items that are already stored in the lowest level of the pyramid. Each internal PE is connected to nine other PEs: one parent, four neighbors on its own level, and four children. Each PE has a constant number of words of memory. The pyramid computer operates in an SIMD mode with uniform addressing and weak uniform communication. Each PE has a mask register that selectively disables PEs.

The analysis in this chapter is much shorter than that of Chapter 5. This is because many of the algorithms presented in that section also operate on pyramid computers. In particular, algorithms for plain mesh connected computers can be run in the lowest level of a pyramid computer. Also, algorithms for mesh plus tree computers can be run on a pyramid computer by using only the vertical connections and the horizontal connections in the base of the pyramid. Some problems that were examined in Chapter 5 will be ignored here, because the best pyramid algorithms are identical to the plain mesh or mesh plus tree algorithms.

7.1 $M \times M$ Convolution

In Section 5.2, an $O(M^2)$ time algorithm was given for performing an $M \times M$ convolution. That same algorithm is the best published algorithm for performing convolutions on pyramid computers. That algorithm moves every pixel in each $M \times M$ window to the PE in the center of the window. The pixels are accessed in a spiral order to limit the communication costs.

It was also mentioned that the same approach can be used to perform many local neighborhood operations on a mesh connected computer. There are some local neighborhood operations, however, that cannot be solved in this manner. For example, median filtering requires that each pixel be replaced by the median gray level in the $M \times M$ window centered on that pixel. Because each PE has only a constant number of words of memory, the median cannot be calculated from the M^2 pixels that pass through each PE. The problem of median filtering on pyramid machines has been studied by a number of authors. In Ref. 242, Tanimoto presents a number of algorithms for solving the problem. The fastest algorithm that Tanimoto presents for a pyramid with a constant number of words of memory per PE requires $O(M^3)$ time. That algorithm uses only the lowest level of the pyramid and could, therefore, be run on a plain mesh connected computer. An $O(M)$ time pyramid algorithm for the same problem is given by Stout in Ref. 233. However, the constant of proportionality in the time analysis of that algorithm is very large, so it is unlikely that it would be used in practice.

7.2 Hough Transform

The Hough transform can be calculated in $O(Q + N^{1/2})$ time on a pyramid by using the $O(Q + N^{1/2})$ time algorithm presented in Section 5.5. Thus, the fastest known Hough transform algorithm for pyramids uses only the lowest level of the pyramid. In Ref. 26, Blanford gives a pyramid algorithm for estimating the locations of peaks in a generalized Hough transform. The generalized Hough transform is similar to the standard Hough transform, except that the image is divided into circular, parabolic, or elliptical bands, as opposed to straight bands. The generalized Hough transform can be used to find circles, parabolas, or ellipses in an image by finding peaks in the parameter space. Because the parameter space has three or more dimensions (depending on the type of bands that are used), it is often impractical to compute the entire parameter space. As a result, algorithms that estimate the locations of peaks in the parameter space are useful.

Blanford's algorithm operates by placing votes (that is, points in the parameter space) into the top of the pyramid in a sequential manner. Therefore, it performs best when there are relatively few votes that are being cast into a relatively large parameter space. The algorithm works by dividing the parameter space into buckets that contain roughly equal numbers of votes. As new votes are cast, the shapes of the buckets are adjusted to maintain a roughly equal number of votes in each. At the end of the procedure, the smallest buckets represent peaks in the parameter space. The pyramid structure is useful because the buckets are maintained in a tree. The root of the tree is located in the top of the pyramid, and the vertical connections in the pyramid are used as links in the tree. Although the horizontal connections are used occasionally, the algorithm would operate nearly as well on a tree of PEs.

7.3 Sorting

The fastest sorting algorithms for pyramids are the $O(N^{1/2})$ time mesh connected computer algorithms presented in Section 5.7. It is clear that this is the best time bound possible for mesh connected computers because their diameter is proportional to $P^{1/2}$, and the case $N = P$ is being considered. Because the pyramid computer has a diameter proportional to $\log P$, it is natural to ask whether an asymptotically faster sorting algorithm is possible on the pyramid. The answer is no, as was proven by Stout.[233] Stout's proof is based on the *minimum bisection width* of the pyramid.

The minimum bisection width of a graph with P nodes is the smallest number of edges that must be removed so that the nodes can be divided into two sets, one of size floor($P/2$) and the other of size ceiling($P/2$), such that there are no edges between nodes in different sets. Thompson has shown that the minimum bisection width of an interconnection network can be used to obtain a lower bound on the amount of time required to sort with that interconnection topology.[247] If a parallel computer with P processors has an interconnection network with a minimum bisection width of W, then sorting P items on that computer (which are stored one per PE both before and after the sort) must require time proportional to P/W (in the worst case). This is because some sorting problem will require that floor($P/2$) items will move from one of the sets of nodes to the other, but only W wires connect the two sets.

Stout showed that the minimum bisection width of a pyramid is proportional to $P^{1/2}$. Specifically, he considered slicing a pyramid with a plane that is perpendicular to the base and to one of the base's sides and that is slightly to one side of the apex. Such a plane divides the PEs into sets of nearly equal size and cuts only $O(P^{1/2})$ wires. Therefore, when $N = P$, some sorting problem will require time that is proportional to $N^{1/2}$. Of course, the same argument applies to the RAW and RAR operations studied in Section 5.8, therefore, pointer-based communication on the pyramid also requires time proportional to $N^{1/2}$.

7.4 Image Connected Component Labeling

In Ref. 162, Miller and Stout present an algorithm for labeling the connected components of a binary image using a pyramid computer. Their algorithm requires $O(N^{1/4})$ time and is similar to the symbolic component labeling algorithm presented in Section 5.9. The algorithm has $O(\log N)$ stages. At the beginning of the i-th stage, the image is divided into $2^i \times 2^i$ pixel windows that have been labeled. During the i-th stage, sets of four adjacent $2^i \times 2^i$ windows are merged to obtain $2^{i+1} \times 2^{i+1}$ windows. The labels for these larger windows are calculated by resolving inconsistencies along the borders of adjacent $2^i \times 2^i$ windows. Because there are only $O(2^i)$ pixels that lie on these borders, the border pixels are moved to a small mesh with $O(2^i)$ PEs. The key to the pyramid algorithm is that the border pixels can be moved to this small mesh by using the vertical connections of the pyramid. Although this algorithm requires only $O(N^{1/4})$ time, the constants of proportionality are large, and it is quite slow for realistic values of N. As a result, the mesh connected computer algorithms presented in Ref. 61 would probably be faster in practice.

7.5 Conclusions for Pyramid Computers

It is clear from the above analysis that most problems can be solved as quickly on a mesh plus tree computer as on a pyramid machine. This is significant because the pyramid machine is more difficult to build than the mesh plus tree computer. Of all of the problems that were examined above, only the median filtering and image-connected component labeling algorithms were asymptotically faster on a pyramid than on a mesh plus tree computer. Furthermore, both of these algorithms are actually quite slow for realistic problem sizes, and the problems are probably best solved by using plain mesh connected computer algorithms.

Although pyramid computers do not seem preferable to mesh plus tree computers based on the problems that have been studied here, it is possible that they are preferable for certain problems. One type of algorithm that is often suggested for pyramid machines consists of analyzing an image at multiple levels of resolution. The lowest level of the pyramid holds the actual image, while the higher levels hold increasingly lower resolution versions of the same image. The lower resolution images can be formed by having each PE store the mean or median of its children's values. Once this data structure has been built, operations can be performed at the appropriate level of resolution and data can be transferred between levels. For instance, in Ref. 241, Tanimoto studies the problem of bright spot detection, where a relatively bright region of the image must be located so that it can be used as a seed for a region-growing operation. The bright spot is found by traveling down the pyramid from the top, and at each step, going to the son of the current PE that has the brightest value. The pixel that is chosen is not guaranteed to be the brightest, but it should be good for region growing because it is relatively bright and has relatively bright pixels nearby. The algorithm takes $O(\log N)$ time.

Like Blanford's Hough transform algorithm discussed in Section 7.2, this bright spot detection algorithm could be run on a mesh plus tree computer. However, there are some algorithms that perform better on pyramids than on mesh plus tree computers. For instance, in Ref. 241, Tanimoto presents an algorithm for region filling that has a good expected case performance. The algorithm makes use of the horizontal connections at all levels of the pyramid.

A particularly interesting result is that sorting and pointer-based communication cannot be performed more quickly (in an asymptotic sense) on a pyramid computer than on a mesh connected computer. As a result, the pyramid computer also seems poorly suited to performing high level, symbolic processing of images. As will be seen in the following chapters, the hypercube and related interconnection networks are better suited to such symbolic processing.

In addition to the pyramid computers examined here, a number of different types of pyramid computers have been proposed. One variation that has been proposed consists of modifying the structure so that some or all of the PEs have more than one parent. Proposals for such modified pyramids can be found in Refs. 3, 4, and 76. Additional information on pyramids can be found in Refs. 71, 127, 211, 225, 239, 240, and 250.

CHAPTER 8

Hypercube Computers

8.1 Introduction to Hypercube Computers

Both the mesh connected computer and the pyramid computer have sufficient near-neighbor connections to perform local neighborhood operations
in an amount of time that is independent of the machine size. In contrast,
algorithms, such as sorting and image-connected component labeling, that
require many long distance data transfers become much slower as the problem and machine sizes increase. The hypercube computer can support large,
global transfers of data very efficiently.

A hypercube computer consists of $P = 2^p$ PEs connected in a rich manner.
The connections can be defined either geometrically or arithmetically. In the
geometric definition, the PEs correspond to corners of a p-dimensional hypercube and the links correspond to the edges of the hypercube. A hypercube
with $P = 2^p$ PEs can be viewed as being two hypercubes with 2^{p-1} PEs each,
with connections between the corresponding corners of the smaller hypercubes. In the arithmetic definition, each PE is assigned a unique index from
0 through $P - 1$. Any two PEs are connected if and only if the binary representations of their indices differ in exactly 1 bit position. Thus, PE X is
connected to all PEs of the form $X^{(i)}$, where $0 \leq i < p$. The geometric and
arithmetic definitions can be reconciled with one another by associating each
of the p dimensions with a unique bit position. The property of having indices
that differ in one bit position is then equivalent to occupying corresponding
corners of two $(p - 1)$-dimensional hypercubes. The selection of which dimension corresponds to which bit position is completely arbitrary. Figure 8.1
shows the layout of a hypercube of 64 processors.

Two types of arguments have been shown for obtaining lower bounds on
the time required to perform global operations, such as sorting and pointer-
based communication. The first argument is that these global operations
must take time proportional to the diameter of the interconnection network
(in the worst case). The diameter of a mesh connected computer is proportional to $P^{1/2}$, while the diameter of the pyramid and hypercube computers is
proportional to $\log P$. The second argument is that if the minimum bisection

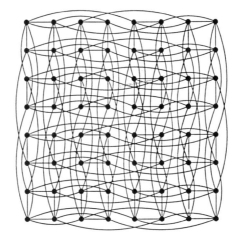

Fig. 8.1. Hypercube interconnection with 64 processors [Seitz, 1985].

width (see Section 7.3) of the interconnection network is W, sorting and pointer-based communication must take time proportional to P/W (in the worst case). The minimum bisection width of a mesh connected computer and of a pyramid is proportional to $P^{1/2}$, while the minimum bisection width of a hypercube is proportional to P.[99]

Combining these two arguments, it is seen that sorting and pointer-based communication with $N = P$ data items requires time proportional to at least $N^{1/2}$ on a mesh connected computer or a pyramid and time proportional to at least $\log N$ on a hypercube. Algorithms that match these lower bounds for mesh connected computers and pyramids have already been shown. Chapter 10 will show that algorithms that nearly match the $\log N$ lower bound for hypercubes can be obtained. However, the problem of whether sorting and pointer-based communication can be performed in time proportional to $\log N$ on the hypercube remains open.

The hypercube's ability to support global operations efficiently does not come for free. Each PE in a hypercube with $P = 2^p$ PEs has connections to p other PEs, so as the number of PEs increases, the degree of (the number of connections to) the PEs also increases. Furthermore, a hypercube has $O(P \log P)$ connections. In contrast, in a mesh connected computer or a pyramid computer, the degree of the PEs is fixed and there are only $O(P)$ connections. As a result, the hypercube computer becomes increasingly difficult to build as larger machines are attempted. Despite this limitation, a number of hypercube computers have been constructed. The remainder of this chapter looks at some of the existing hypercube machines.

8.2 The Cosmic Cube

The Cosmic Cube is a six-dimensional hypercube that was completed in 1983 at Caltech.[222] Each of the 64 PEs contains an Intel 8086 processor, an Intel 8087 floating-point coprocessor, 128 Kbytes of RAM, and 8K bytes of ROM. The PEs operate independently in an MIMD mode. The Cosmic Cube was designed primarily for solving scientific problems such as those arising in physics quantum chemistry, fluid mechanics, and seismology.

The Cosmic Cube uses a distributed operating system to support a process-oriented view of computation. The programmer views a program as consisting of a number of processes (sequential programs) that communicate with one another through a message passing protocol. The Cosmic Cube is programmed in traditional high-level languages, such as Pascal and C, that have been extended to include the message passing primitives. The programmer can choose to assign processes to PEs and perform all communications using only the direct physical links between PEs. Alternatively, the programmer may adopt a more abstract view of the machine and allow the operating system to allocate processes to PEs and to perform the routing of messages between processes. Messages are physically transmitted using 64-bit packets, but the details of the packet size and routing can be hidden from the programmer.

8.3 The NCUBE

In 1985, the NCUBE Corporation introduced a set of hypercube computers.[101,173,182] The largest computer, called the NCUBE/ten, contains 1,024 PEs arranged in a ten-dimensional hypercube. Each PE, which occupies a single custom chip, is a 32-bit floating-point processor. The custom processor chips are fabricated using a 2-micron NMOS process. Each chip contains approximately 160,000 transistors, has 68 pins, and is capable of operating with a 100-ns cycle time. A single PE is capable of performing approximately 500,000 single-precision floating-point operations per second. Each PE has 16 32-bit registers on the chip and an additional 128K bytes of RAM located on 6 memory chips.

A set of one processor chip and six memory chips forms a node of the hypercube. A six-dimensional hypercube of 64 nodes is placed on a single board. The NCUBE/ten consists of 16 such processor boards, plus up to 8 I/O boards. Each I/O board has 128 bidirectional channels to 128 PEs in the hypercube. Thus, it is possible to have a separate I/O channel for each PE. In certain situations, it is possible to transfer approximately 720M bytes of data per second into the hypercube.

The NCUBE/ten is an MIMD machine. A common mode of operation is called the SPMD (single-program, multiple-data) mode. In this mode, each

PE has a copy of the same program. Thus, like in an SIMD machine, the processors have the same instructions. However, different PEs can perform different branches of if-statements at the same time, thus, improving the efficiency. The primary strengths of the NCUBE/ten are its very powerful processors, its large amount of memory per processor, its fast I/O operations, and its MIMD capabilities. Even though it does not have as many processors as some other machines, such as the MPP or the Connection Machine CM-2, the processors are far more powerful that the bit-serial processors present in those machines. As a result, the NCUBE/ten is comparable in power to those larger machines.

8.4 The Intel iPSC

Intel has created a hypercube computer that is designed primarily for scientific and engineering applications.[13,42,178] The second generation offering, called the iPSC/2, was introduced in December 1987. The iPSC/2 is an MIMD computer in which each node consists of a 32-bit Intel 80386 microprocessor, an 80387 floating-point coprocessor, a 64K byte static RAM cache for data and code, from 1M to 16M bytes of dynamic RAM, and a router. A node occupies a single board. Hypercubes with up to 128 nodes are available.

The 80386 processor runs at 16MHz and is rated at 4 MIPS. The 80387 coprocessor provides ANSI/IEEE standard floating-point operations. An optional Weitek 1167 coprocessor can be installed on the same board to provide the same floating-point operations at a greater speed. Also, an optional vector coprocessor board can be attached to a node board for even higher performance.

All hypercube communication operations are performed by the separate router unit present in each node. The routers are implemented in CMOS programmable gate-arrays. Connections between routers are logically full-duplex, bit-serial channels. However, the physical implementation of a channel consists of four separate wires, a pair of which are unidirectional in one direction and a pair of which are unidirectional in the other. Each pair of unidirectional wires consists of a data wire and a strobe wire. A transition on the strobe wire indicates that a bit is present on the data wire. Communication in the iPSC/2 is circuit-switched, therefore, an entire path from the source node to the destination node is reserved before data transmission begins. The strobe wires along this path are electrically connected so that the strobe signals form a clock for the associated data path. This system allows the data to be sent in a completely synchronous manner without having to perform arbitration between the clocks of the nodes along the message path. Status information, such as whether or not the destination node has sufficient buffer space, is routed from the destination node to the source node along the same path.

In order to send a message, the source node creates a routing probe that specifies the destination node. Each bit of the routing probe corresponds to one bit of the index of the destination node. The probe has a 1 in those bit positions that differ between the current node and the destination node and a 0 in the other positions. For example, a message that is being sent from node number 69 (binary 01000101) that is being sent to node number 33 (binary 00100001) has a probe of 01100100. Thus, each bit in the probe corresponds to a dimension of the hypercube, and the bit is a 1 if and only if the corresponding dimension should be traversed.

The probe is routed to the destination node by crossing the dimensions that have 1s in the probe in order from the least significant to the most significant dimension. This routing algorithm, which is known as the e-cube algorithm,[143,236] guarantees freedom from deadlock in routing messages. However, note that the e-cube algorithm assigns a unique path to each message that depends only on the addresses of the source and destination nodes. As a result, the path that a message takes cannot be selected to avoid collisions with existing messages. Also, a faulty router that happens to be on the selected path cannot be avoided.

8.5 The Connection Machine

The *Connection Machine* is a very large machine built by Thinking Machines Corporation that became commercially available in 1986.[106,164] The initial release, called the CM-1, has 64K PEs that are interconnected as a 12-dimensional hypercube, each node of which contains 16 PEs. In addition to the hypercube connections, the 64K PEs are connected in a 256×256 mesh. The machine operates in an SIMD mode under the direction of a host computer that issues control instructions to the PEs.

The CM-1 is constructed from custom VLSI chips, each of which contains 16 PEs and 1 router. The chips use CMOS technology and have approximately 50,000 devices each in an area of 1 cm^2. Each chip has 68 pins and can operate with a 250-ns clock cycle. Associated with each chip are four $4K \times 4$ static RAM chips. Thirty-two of these 5-chip processor, router and memory units are placed on a single printed circuit board. Sixteen of these printed circuit boards are plugged into a backplane, and two backplanes are combined to form a single rack. Four racks are combined to create the entire 64K PE machine. The machine is approximately cube-shaped and is about 4 feet on a side.

The design of a single PE is shown in Figure 8.2. Each PE contains a bit-serial processor, eight 1-bit registers, and 4K bits of memory located off-chip. A single processing operation in a PE consists of accessing two bits from the RAM and one bit from one of the registers, using the processor to compute two boolean functions of the three input bits, and storing one of the

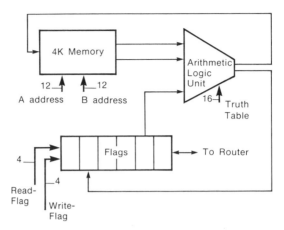

Fig. 8.2. Connection Machine processor design [Hillis, 1985].

result bits in RAM and the other result bit in a register. The processor is capable of computing any of the $2^{16} = 64K$ boolean functions from 3 inputs to 2 outputs. Unlike the MPP and PAPIA, the PEs in the Connection Machine do not have shift registers, therefore, all intermediate results of bit-serial arithmetic operations must be stored in RAM. One of the registers is used as a mask register to selectively disable PEs. The CM-1 uses uniform addressing.

In addition to the processing instruction discussed above, the PEs are able to perform three types of communication instructions. The first type uses the mesh connections to perform near-neighbor communications. The second type uses the hypercube connections to communicate between hypercube neighbors. The third type of communication uses the router to send messages between arbitrary PEs. This type of communication provides a high-level interface to the machine that hides the hypercube structure from the programmer.

The CM-1 is designed primarily for **artificial intelligence** (AI) applications that are written in a high-level language that is an extension of Lisp, called CmLisp. The programmer of such an application has an abstract view of the machine that hides the details of the hypercube interconnection structure. The CmLisp programmer specifies parallel operations that are to be performed on list data structures. Such operations involve a large number of pointer operations that are executed in parallel. These operations exhibit irregular long distance communication paths.

The purpose of the routers is to implement such communications in an efficient manner using the hypercube connections. The routers deliver message packets that have 12-bit headers specifying the destination address. As was the case for the iPSC/2, the header consists of the exclusive-or of the source and destination addresses. Thus, each bit with a value of 1 in the header indicates a need for a transfer in the corresponding dimension in the hypercube.

Routing is performed in cycles. At the beginning of a cycle, each message that is being routed is stored at a single router. The routing is performed in a uniform manner by checking each of the 12 dimensions in the hypercube in order. For each dimension, the routers check their message buffers for messages with headers indicating that they must move in the given direction. If no such message is found, that router is idle while the transfer is being started by the other routers. Although initiating message transfers across different dimensions is sequential, the transfers for a given dimension are started before the transfers for the previous dimensions have completed, so multiple dimensions can be active simultaneously. As a result of this pipelining of successive dimensions, parts of a single message that is crossing multiple dimensions can be in many different routers during a routing cycle. However, at the end of a routing cycle, the messages are again stored in a single router. While messages normally only move closer to their destinations, a provision has been made for moving messages away from their destinations when a router's buffer becomes full.

Note that unlike the routing algorithm used by the iPSC/2, the routing algorithm used by the CM-1 is adaptive. Specifically, the path that a message takes can be affected by the presence of other messages. As a result, messages can modify their paths to avoid congestion. However, because of the adaptive nature of the routing algorithm, no proof of freedom from deadlock has been given.

The details of the routing algorithm and hardware can have profound and unexpected effects on the performance of algorithms. In particular, an algorithm that is designed to use only direct connections in a hypercube computer can perform very poorly when it is mapped in the natural manner (virtual PE i to physical PE i) to the CM-1. This is because the 16 PEs per router will all attempt to communicate across the same single dimension. The router can only send one of them across that dimension at a time, so 16 complete cycles through the 12 dimensions will be required. On the other hand, if the algorithm is mapped so that communicating PEs are far apart in the hypercube, each message will have a large number of dimensions to cross. Therefore, many of the 16 messages starting at each router will be able to be sent out during the first cycle of routing the 12 dimensions, and only a few such cycles will be required.

One of the greatest weaknesses of the CM-1 was its performance on floating-point operations. Although the machine was originally designed for artificial intelligence applications, there was more demand for a high-performance parallel machine for scientific applications. In order to meet these needs, a newer version of the machine, called CM-2, was created. CM-2 has the same custom PE chips as used in CM-1, but it also has a 32-bit floating-point processor associated with each set of 32 bit-serial processors. In order to use this floating-point processor, the data from the bit-serial processors must be reformatted. This is because the set of 32-bit serial processors produces 32 32-bit numbers 1 bit position at a time. In other words, at any one time, a single-bit position from 32 different numbers is produced. Of course, the 32-bit floating-point processor must access a single-32-bit number at a time. The reformatting of the data is performed by a special interface unit that can be accessed in either manner.

The other significant improvements in the CM-2 are support for performing independent addressing and an increase in each PE's off-chip memory from 4K bits to 64K bits. The CM-2 dropped the mesh interconnection network of the CM-1, because mesh operations can be performed equally efficiently on a hypercube (the two-dimensional mesh is a subgraph of the hypercube).

CHAPTER 9

Hypercube-Derived Computers

9.1 Introduction to Hypercube-Derived Computers

A serious difficulty with the hypercube topology is its log P degree. Because technological constraints limit the number of connections that are possible from any one processor, the number of processors that can be connected in a hypercube is limited. Furthermore, if a single-node chip is to be used in different size hypercubes, the chip must have enough connections for the largest hypercube in which it will be used. Therefore, when the chip is used in smaller hypercubes, some of the connections will be wasted.

Several topologies have been proposed that have many of the advantages of the hypercube, and yet, have a constant degree. Four of these topologies, namely the shuffle-exchange (SE),[166,221,232] de Bruijn (dB),[21,210] cube-connected cycles (CCC),[196] and butterfly (BF),[22,251] will be considered here. All four of these networks are well-suited to performing two classes of parallel computations known as *ascend* and *descend* algorithms.[196] First, ascend and descend algorithms will be examined, and then, how they can be implemented on the four topologies mentioned above will be studied. Finally, multistage, switch-based interconnection networks that are also related to the hypercube will be studied.

An ascend algorithm manipulates an array A containing N items, numbered 0 through $N - 1$. Let $n = \log N$. An ascend algorithm has n stages, numbered 0 through $n - 1$, where stage i performs calculations between pairs of array locations that differ in bit i. Class descend algorithms are identical, except the bit positions are processed in the opposite order, therefore, stage i of a descend algorithm performs calculations between array locations that differ in bit $n - i$. Class ascend and descend algorithms are often produced when a problem is solved in a divide-and-conquer manner where each problem is divided into two subproblems of half the size. Preparata and Vuillemin identified quite a few algorithms that are class ascend or descend algorithms or are composed entirely of subroutines that are class ascend or descend algorithms.[196] Their examples include the bitonic merge and bitonic sort, the radix-2 FFT, the simulation of a Benes network and matrix multiplication.

When $N = P$, it is clear that the communication for any ascend or descend algorithm can be implemented on a hypercube with weak uniform communication in log N steps by simply storing each array location i in processor i. How the communication for ascend and descend algorithms can also be implemented in O(log N) time on several constant degree processor-based networks will now be studied.

9.2 Shuffle-Exchange Computers

In an SE computer, the processors are numbered 0 through $P - 1$, where P is a power of 2. Let $p = \log P$. Each processor X is connected to processor $X^{(0)}$ (see Section 1.2), processor $(X_{(p-2)}, X_{(p-3)}, \ldots, X_{(0)}, X_{(p-1)})$, and processor $(X_{(0)}, X_{(p-1)}, \ldots, X_{(1)})$. These connections are called the exchange, the shuffle, and the unshuffle connections, respectively. First consider implementing an ascend algorithm on an SE computer when $N = P$. Initially, each array location i is stored in processor i. The exchange links connect pairs of array locations that differ in bit 0, so the communication for bit 0 can be performed in constant time. Next, each array location is transferred along an unshuffle connection. At this point, each array location X is stored in processor $(X_{(0)}, X_{(p-1)}, \ldots, X_{(1)})$. As a result, the exchange links now provide a connection between array locations that differ in bit 1. This process of alternating the use of exchange and unshuffle connections is repeated log N times in order to implement the communication for the entire ascend algorithm in 2 log N steps.[232] A similar approach can be used to implement the communication for a descend algorithm in 2 log N steps. Specifically, array location i is again stored in processor i. Then, a series of log N stages, each consisting of a shuffle followed by an exchange, is used to access pairs of array locations differing in bits $n - 1$ through 0.

9.3 de Bruijn Computers

A dB computer can be defined for any value of P that is a power of 2. In a dB computer with P processors, each processor X is connected to processor $(0, X_{(p-1)}, X_{(p-2)}, \ldots, X_{(1)})$, processor $(1, X_{(p-1)}, X_{(p-2)}, \ldots, X_{(1)})$, processor $(X_{(p-2)}, X_{(p-3)}, \ldots, X_{(0)}, 0)$, and processor $(X_{(p-2)}, X_{(p-3)}, \ldots, X_{(0)}, 1)$. The first two connections will be called the forward connections, and the last two connections, the backward connections. The communication for an ascend algorithm with $N = 2P$ is implemented in log N steps on a dB computer as follows. Initially, each array location X is stored in processor floor$(X/2)$. Pairs of array locations that differ in bit 0 are stored in the same processor, therefore, no communication is required for bit 0. Next, the two array locations in each processor are transferred along the forward connections, with the even array location going to the processor with a 0 as the most significant bit and the odd array location going to the processor with a 1 as the most significant bit. At this point, pairs of array locations that differ in bit 1 are stored in the same processor. The entire ascend algorithm is implemented by repeating this procedure log N times. Descend algorithms are implemented in an analogous manner with the backward connections. It is clear that the dB computer and the SE computer implement ascend and descend algorithms in a very similar manner. In fact, there is a simple relationship between the two topologies. Specifically, if the pairs of processors in an SE computer with P processors are merged, a dB computer with $P/2$ processors is obtained.

9.4 Cube-Connected Cycles Computers

The simplest type of CCC computer has P processors where $P = k2^k$ and $k = 2^j$. Each processor is assigned a unique pair of the form (C, R) where C is in the range 0 through $k - 1$ and R is in the range 0 through $2^k - 1$. The processors can be viewed as forming a 2^k by k array, with processor (C, R) in row R and column C. Each processor is connected to its neighbors to the left and right (with a wraparound connection from the rightmost column to the leftmost column). In addition, in each column i, the pairs of processors that are in rows that differ in bit position i are connected. More formally, each processor (C, R) is connected to processor $(C + 1 \bmod k, R)$, processor $(C - 1 \bmod k, R)$ and process $(C, R^{(C)})$. These three connections are called the forward, backward, and lateral connections, respectively. The communication for any ascend algorithm with $N = P$ can be performed in approximately $6 \log N$ steps on a CCC. Each array location i is initially stored in processor (C, R), where $C = i \bmod k$ and $R = \text{floor}\left(\dfrac{i}{k}\right)$. Note that array locations with binary representations that differ only in the log K least significant bits are stored in the same row of the CCC. As a result, the horizontal (forward and backward) connections are used for these bit positions. Specifically, in order to perform the communication for bit i, $0 \leq i < j$, each array location with a 0 in bit i is sent across the forward connections 2^i times. At this point, the pairs of array locations that differ in bit i are stored in the same processor. After performing the processing for bit i, the shifted array locations are sent back to their original positions by using the backward connections 2^i times. As a result, the communication for bit i, $0 \leq i < j$, requires 2^{i+1} steps and the total communication required by the j least significant bits is approximately $2k$.

Communication for bits j through $k + j - 1$ is performed in a pipelined manner. Note that in column 0, pairs of array locations that differ in bit j are connected by lateral connections. As a result, bit j communication for array locations in column 0 is performed next, while array locations in the remaining columns are idle. Next, each array location (from each of the columns) is transferred to the next column by using the forward links. At this point, the array locations that are currently in column 1 use the lateral connections to perform their bit $j + 1$ communication (they have already performed their bit j communication), the array locations that are currently in column 0 use the lateral connections to perform their bit j communication, and the remaining columns are idle. Next, each array location is transferred over a forward link. Then, the array locations in column 2 perform their bit $j + 2$ communication, those in column 1 perform their bit $j + 1$ communication, those in column 0 perform their bit j communication, and the remaining columns are idle.

This process of shifting the data with the forward connections and using the lateral connections is repeated until all of the communication has been completed. Each array location begins its bit j communication when it first reaches column 0 and then performs its communication for the remaining bits in the remaining columns. Each stage of this procedure requires two steps (one for the lateral communication and one for the forward communication), and a total of $2k - 1$ such steps are required (k for the array locations originally in column 0 and $k - 1$ to flush the pipe), so approximately $4k$ steps are required for bits j through $k + j - 1$. The entire ascend algorithm, thus, takes approximately $6k$, or approximately $6 \log N$, communication steps. Once again, descend algorithms can be implemented by reversing the procedure used for ascend algorithms.

9.5 Butterfly Computers

The BF topology is a degree 4 interconnection pattern that is closely related to the CCC. As was the case with the CCC, a BF computer has P processors, where $P = k2^k$ and $k = 2^j$. Again, each processor is assigned a unique pair of the form (C, R), where $0 \le C < k$ and $0 \le R < 2^k$, and the processors are viewed as forming a 2^k by k array, with processor (C, R) in row R and column C. Each processor (C, R) is connected to processor $(C + 1 \bmod k, R)$, processor $(C + 1 \bmod k, R^{(C)})$, processor $(C - 1 \bmod k, R)$, and processor $(C - 1 \bmod k, R^{(C-1 \bmod k)})$. Ascend and descend algorithms are implemented on BF computers in a manner analogous to their implementation on CCC computers. The communication for an ascend or descend algorithm with $N = 2P$ can be performed in approximately $6 \log N$ steps on a BF computer with strong half-duplex communication.

9.6 Switch-Based Computers

In addition to the processor-based networks that are derived from the hypercube topology, there are a number of multistage switch-based networks that are related to hypercubes. One of the most important of these switch-based networks is the Omega network.[145] Assume that the number of processors,

P, is a power of 2 and let $p = \log P$. An Omega network can be constructed as follows. First, arrange the P processors in a column and number the processors 0 through $P - 1$ from top to bottom. Next, create p columns (stages) of 2×2 switches, consisting of $P/2$ switches each, and place these columns of switches to the right of the column of processors. Within each column of switches, number the inputs to the switches from 0 through $P - 1$ from top to bottom and number the outputs of the switches from 0 through $P - 1$ from top to bottom. Then add connections between each adjacent column (of processor or switches) according to the shuffle permutation. That is, each processor (or switch output) numbered X is connected to the switch input numbered $(X_{(p-2)}, X_{(p-3)}, \ldots, X_{(0)}, X_{(p-1)})$. Finally, add "wraparound" connections between each output i from the last column of switches and processor i.

Routing in an Omega network corresponds to a descend algorithm. More specifically, the binary representation of the destination address is examined in order from most significant bit to least significant bit, and these bits give the output ports to be selected in each of the columns of switches. A 0 bit corresponds to selecting the upper output port, while a 1 bit corresponds to selecting the lower output port. Thus, if the most significant bit of the destination is a 1 (respectively, 0), the lower (respectively, upper) output port of the switch in the first column is selected. It is clear that any processor can send a message to any other processor using this routing algorithm and that every message must pass through the same number of switches (namely p).

The description here has focused on the use of 2×2 switches, but it is possible to create Omega networks using larger switches. In general, if $B \times B$ switches are used, the number of processors P is a power of B, the number switches per column is P/B, and there are $\log P/\log B$ columns of switches. The connections between successive columns form a base B shuffle, which performs a left circular shift of the base B representation of the port (or processor) number.

The Omega network provides exactly one route from each processor to each other processor. As a result, if processor A is attempting to send a message to processor A', while processor B is attempting to send a message to processor B', and if the unique path from A to A' intersects the unique path from B to B', the messages may collide with one another. In general, a significant amount of congestion can occur when attempting to implement a permutation on an Omega network. Fortunately, there is another related network that is capable of implementing every permutation without collisions. This network, which is called the Benes network,[20,260] is essentially two copies of an Omega network placed back-to-back. More precisely, a base-2 Benes network with $P = 2^p$ processors consists of $2p - 1$ columns of $P/2$ switches each. Each of the first p columns is connected with an unshuffle permutation (which is the inverse of the shuffle permutation) and each of the last p columns (including the processors) is connected with a shuffle permutation. Therefore, routing through the first p columns corresponds to an ascend algorithm and routing through the last p columns corresponds to a descend algorithm. The fact that the Benes network can implement every permutation without collisions and an algorithm for setting the switches so as to accomplish this are given in Section 10.6.1, which discusses static permutations on hypercube computers.

A number of machines with multistage networks based on the Omega or Benes network have been created. The GF11[19] is a parallel computer that was built in IBM Yorktown for solving specialized physics applications, such as quantum chromodynamics. These calculations consist of regular and repetitive calculations and permutations of data between the processors. In order to implement these calcuations efficiently, an SIMD architecture with a Benes multistage interconnection network was selected. The Benes network is based on 24×24 (rather than 2×2) switches, thus, decreasing the number of stages that are required. In fact, the network consists of only three stages, each of which has 24 switches, thus, providing 576 inputs and 576 outputs (although the current implementation consists of approximately 250 processors). Because the communication patterns are static (i.e., known at compile time), the switch settings can be calculated in advance and the network can implement the desired communication without collisions. Each processor consists of two 32-bit IEEE standard floating-point multipliers and two ALUs located on a single board.

Another recently announced parallel computer is the SP-1 from IBM. The SP-1 is based on the Vulcan prototype parallel computer that was developed by the IBM Research Division. The SP-1 consists of RS/6000 processors, which are connected by an Omega network consisting of 4×4 switches. The network has extra stages to allow multiple paths between each source-destination pair. In addition, each processor has two output ports and two input ports, thus, increasing the bandwidth available to and from the network. Routing is performed with packets, each of which takes a predetermined path from the source to the destination. Initially, the SP-1 will contain up to 64 processors, but the architecture is designed to scale to larger sizes.

The SP-1 is designed to support multiple users, each of whom can access one or more processors. In particular, the processors are logically divided into two pools, one of which is for parallel jobs and the other of which is for sequential jobs. A user can access a processor in the sequential pool and use the processor as a remote workstation, or the user can request a set of processors from the parallel pool and run a parallel program. Because the set of processors from the parallel pool that are allocated to the user depend on the other users of the system, and because the distance in the multistage network between any two processors is the same, the user is encouraged to view the machine as a fully connected set of processors. Thus, the user is aware of the fact that accessing data that are local to a processor is faster than accessing data that are stored in a remote processor. However, the time required to access data from any two different remote processors is viewed as being identical. This fully connected model simplifies programming and aids in the portability of parallel applications at the cost of sacrificing the possibility of fine-tuning the communication to match the interconnection network.

Another recent machine introduced in the market is the *Connection Machine* CM-5, by Thinking Machines Corporation.[151] This computer differs from its predecessors, the CM-1 and CM-2, in several fundamental ways. The Connection Machine 5 is an MIMD computer hosting from 32 to 16K SPARC processors that are interconnected via three different networks each serving data, control, and diagnostics. The basic architecture of the data network is a multistage network called a "fat-tree." The fat-tree network is similar to the Omega network, but has two major differences. First, the processors are connected only to the first stage of switches and all of the connections are bidirectional. Thus, instead of routing through the stages from left to right and then using the wraparound connections (as is done in the Omega network), routing is performed from left to right through some (variable) number of stages, at which point the packet reverses direction and goes from right to left to its destination. Second, the stages farthest from the processors contain fewer switches. This decreased number of switches per stage lowers the bandwidth of the network, but saves costs. Packet routing on this network is accomplished by making pseudorandom choices while routing from left to right, and then using the destination address to select the output port while routing from right to left. The use of pseudorandom paths breaks the regularity of the traffic, thus, decreasing the likelihood that a communication pattern with a large number of collisions will be encountered.

One of the roles of the control network is to provide efficient interprocessor synchronization mechanisms. This feature of the control network makes the computer suitable to support loosely synchronous models of execution, such as those arising from the implementation of data parallel programming languages. The control network also provides some important primitives such as reduction, broadcasting, parallel prefix. The CM-5 departs from the customized processor approach followed in the CM-1 and CM-2 by introducing a general purpose microprocessor in its architecture. Furthermore, the machine has some hardware facility to provide for fast processor synchronization that allows SIMD operation even though the architecture is MIMD.

9.7 Conclusions for Hypercube-Derived Computers

From the above time bounds, it is clear that the degree 4 processor-based networks (the dB and BF) offer significantly better performance than the respective degree 3 processor-based networks (the SE and CCC) on ascend and descend algorithms. Also, the networks without a row and column structure (the SE and dB) are faster on ascend and descend algorithms. This is because in a network with a row and column structure (a CCC or a BF), the computations within rows are performed on a loop interconnection network.

Furthermore, the networks with a row and column structure are naturally defined only for very special sizes (although the definition of the CCC can be extended to cover any size that is a power of 2 (Ref. 196) at the price of increasing the constants in the running time of ascend and descend algorithms). As a result, the dB network seems to be an excellent candidate for an interconnection network.

However, there is one advantage that the CCC and BF topologies have over the SE and dB topologies, namely, their regularity. In a CCC or BF network, the topology appears the same to each processor. In contrast, in an SE or dB network the topology appears different from different processors. For example, in an SE network, most processors are connected to three different processors, but processors numbered 0 and $P - 1$ are both connected to only one other processor (because their shuffle and unshuffle connections map to themselves). Fortunately, there are ways to decompose the dB topology into identical components, each of which has only a small number of connections to other components.[47] Such a decomposition allows large dB computers to be constructed from a collection of identical chips or boards.

Up to this point the focus has been on ascend and descend algorithms, but other algorithms can be implemented efficiently on these four constant degree topologies. One such class of algorithms is the *bit-block* algorithms.[51] Bit-block algorithms generalize ascend and descend algorithms in two ways. First, while ascend and descend algorithms perform communication for all of the bits in order, bit-block algorithms allow communication to be performed for bits that are out of order (at some additional cost). Second, while ascend and descend algorithms perform communication between pairs of array locations (which differ in a single-bit position), bit-block algorithms perform communication between larger sets of array locations (which differ in some set of bit positions). As long as the sets of communicating array locations are no larger than the number of array locations per processor, bit-block algorithms can be implemented efficiently.

One complication that arises when implementing bit-block algorithms is the fact that more communication may be required for some bit positions than for others. For example, consider an algorithm that performs communication between pairs of array locations that differ in a single bit position, and further assume that communication is only required for a small number of the least significant bit positions. This is not a problem on the SE or dB topologies, but on a CCC or BF machine, all of this communication is between processors that lie on the same row. Because the connections within a row are not very rich (they form a loop), this communication could be prohibitively expensive. Fortunately, it has been shown that it is possible to run bit-block algorithms on CCC and BF machines within a small constant factor of their running times on an SE or dB machine.[51] In fact, a much more general connection between these four topologies has been proven. Specifically, it has been shown that any computation on one of these networks can be performed on any other of these networks with only a constant factor slowdown.[220]

Although the hypercube-derived topologies, in general, and the dB topology, in particular, appear to be excellent candidates for interconnection networks, they have not yet been used for many actual machines. One system has been built of 16 Transputer processors arranged in a shuffle-shift topology (which is closely related to the SE topology).[219] Given the many advantages of these topologies, it seems likely that they will be more common in the future.

CHAPTER 10

Communication Primitives for Hypercube Computers

This chapter presents and analyzes a number of algorithms for performing basic communication operations on hypercubes and hypercube-derived computers. All of the operations will be implemented on what is called a plain hypercube. A plain hypercube consists of $P = 2^p$ PEs arranged in a p-dimensional hypercube. The plain hypercube operates in an SIMD mode with uniform addressing and communication. A single communication operation consists of exchanging data between PEs along a single hypercube dimension. Each PE has a mask register that allows the selective disabling of PEs.

Although all of the problems will be solved on a plain hypercube, a number of other types of computers will also be considered. One other type, which will be called a hypercube with independent addressing, is identical to the plain hypercube computer, except each node contains a larger amount of memory and has the ability to perform independent addressing. Another type, which will be called a hypercube with independent communication, is identical to the plain hypercube computer, except different PEs can communicate across different dimensions simultaneously. Still, each PE in a hypercube with independent communication can only send a single message along a single connection at any given time. Finally, algorithms will be given for the four processor-based hypercube-derived topologies presented in the last chapter. Unless stated otherwise, each processor will be assumed to have $O(N/P)$ words of memory if $N \geq P$ and a constant amount of memory if $N < P$.

10.1 Simulating Larger Machines

Algorithms for the case $N = P$ will be given for all of the communication primitives. Of course, in practice, it is common for N to be larger than P. In this case, it is possible to use the $N = P$ algorithm by simulating a machine with N processors. This is done on a plain hypercube by assigning a subcube of N/P virtual processors to each real processor. This technique produces a simulation of an N processor plain hypercube on a P processor plain hypercube with a factor of N/P slowdown.[83] An analogous technique can also be used to simulate an N processor hypercube-derived computer on a P processor one with a factor of N/P slowdown.[83] It is sometimes possible to reduce the factor of N/P slowdown by modifying the algorithm that is used.

10.2 Simulating Mesh Connected Computers

In Chapter 5, mesh connected computers were shown to be efficient in performing many image and matrix operations. If a mesh connected computer can be simulated with a hypercube or hypercube-derived computer, those same algorithms can be used on these other topologies.

In order to perform the simulation, a mapping must be established from the PEs in the mesh connected computer to the PEs in the hypercube or hypercube-derived computer. The PEs in the mesh connected computer are called virtual PEs and the PEs in the hypercube or hypercube-derived computer are called real PEs. One very natural mapping of virtual PEs to real PEs is to assign virtual PE (i, j) to real PE $iP^{1/2} + j$. This corresponds to a row-major ordering of the mesh connected computer.

While this ordering seems very natural, there is another ordering that is useful. In that ordering, which will be called the Gray ordering, the rows and columns of the mesh connected computer are labeled with Gray codes.[78] Such a Gray code is a list of the integers 0 through $P^{1/2} - 1$ that is arranged so that consecutive integers differ in exactly 1 bit position. Let Gray (i) be the i-th element of a Gray code. The Gray order of virtual PE (i, j) is then defined as Gray $(i)P^{1/2} + $ Gray (j).

In order to evaluate the usefulness of these two orderings, it is necessary to examine how they determine the connections between virtual PEs. It can be shown that virtual PEs that are horizontally or vertically adjacent in the mesh are assigned to connected real PEs when the Gray ordering is used, but they may not be assigned to connected real PEs when the row-major ordering is used. As a result, the Gray ordering offers the possibility of efficiently simulating a mesh connected computer. In fact, when the virtual PEs are assigned according to the Gray ordering, a hypercube with independent communication can simulate a plain mesh connected computer with no loss of speed.

However, there is a difficulty when simulating a mesh connected computer with a plain hypercube computer. Consider, for example, simulating the right-shift operation of a mesh connected computer. Assuming the virtual PEs are assigned to the real PEs according to the Gray ordering, the hypercube computer has a direct link for performing the right shift. However, the links that perform the right shift belong to different dimensions of the hypercube. Because communication can proceed across only one dimension at a time, a plain hypercube computer requires log P operations to implement a single operation of a plain mesh connected computer. A similar problem occurs when using the Gray ordering to simulate a mesh connected computer on a hypercube-derived computer.

A plain hypercube computer, or a hypercube-derived computer, can also implement a single operation of a plain mesh connected computer with $\log P$ operations when the virtual PEs are assigned according to the row-major ordering. As a result, the simpler row-major ordering is as efficient as the Gray ordering for these topologies. Because of these considerations, in the following discussion, it will be assumed that matrices and images are loaded in Gray order when using a hypercube with independent communication and in row-major order otherwise. It should be noted that these two storage techniques can be exchanged rather easily. In particular, a matrix or image can be moved from the Gray order to the row-major order (or vice-versa) in $O(\log P)$ time on any of these topologies by using the algorithms presented in Section 10.6.

Although the simple technique of using a Gray ordering to store a mesh does not yield an efficient simulation of a mesh connected computer on the hypercube-derived computers, it turns out that more sophisticated techniques do yield an asymptotically efficient simulation. Koch et al. have shown the surprising result that a butterfly computer (and by the results of Section 9.6,[220] any hypercube-derived computer) with P processors can simulate a mesh connected computer with P processors with only a constant factor slowdown.[133] The constant of proportionality in the running time of this simulation was not given, but the algorithm is quite complex and, therefore, not of great practical interest.

10.3 Data-Independent Parallel Prefix

The parallel prefix operation is one of the most frequently used operations in parallel computing.[11,29,45,46,62,51,80,87,106,116,135,136,142,157] Parallel prefix operations can be used to extract information from sets of lists of data, to handle the scheduling of parallel processors, to reorganize data sets so that they can be manipulated more efficiently, and to evaluate arithmetic expressions. As a result, different versions of the parallel prefix operation have been proposed as fundamental operations in a number of models of parallel computers. Two versions of the parallel prefix problem will be considered in this section, namely, the scan and the segmented scan problems. A third version, the data-dependent parallel prefix problem, will be examined in Section 10.10.

10.3.1 Scan

The input to the scan problem is an array $A = A(0), A(1), \ldots, A(N-1)$ consisting of N data items and an associative binary operator "$+$" with identity 0. The problem is to compute, for each i, $0 \leq i \leq N-1$, the value $A(0) + A(1) + \cdots + A(i - 1)$. The value $A(0) + A(1) + \cdots + A(i - 1)$ is called the "plus reduction" of the items $A(0), A(1), \ldots, A(i - 1)$. Blelloch has proposed adding the scan operation as a unit time operation to the EREW PRAM model.[29]

The scan problem can be solved with an ascend routine followed by a descend routine (see Chapter 9). The algorithm that will be described here is based on the algorithm presented by Blelloch.[28] The first half of the algorithm calculates the reductions of successively larger blocks of consecutive data items, and the second half of the algorithm uses the results obtained in the first half to calculate the reductions of each of the prefixes. The algorithm can be viewed as creating a complete binary tree where the leaf nodes are the original N data items. The first half of the algorithm performs a bottom up sweep through this tree with each node calculating the plus reduction of its two children. Each node in the tree stores the value passed up from its left child. The second half of the algorithm performs a top down sweep through the tree. During the second half, each node receives a value from its parent (the root of the tree receives the value 0). The node then passes this value to its left child and it passes $X + Y$ to its right child, where S is the value passed up from the left child during the first half and Y is the value received from the parent during the second half. The values received at the leaves are the desired reductions.

The details of how this scan algorithm can be implemented on a plain hypercube or a hypercube-derived computer when $N = P$ will now be considered. It will be assumed that there is an array of N records, each of which has a value, child, and sibchild field. The original data values are placed in the value fields, and the other fields are initialized to 0. The child field will be used to store the value passed up from the left child during the first half of the algorithm, and the sibchild field will be used to store the value from the left child of the node's sibling. The first half has $\log N$ stages, numbered 0 through $\log N - 1$. Let X and Y be a pair of processors that differ only in bit position i and assume that X is the lower numbered processor. During stage i, Y. sibchild is assigned X. child, X. child is assigned X. value, and then X. value is assigned X. value $+ Y$. value. Before beginning the second half, the value field in record 0 is set to 0. The second half has $\log N$ stages that are numbered $\log N - 1$ down through 0. During stage i, Y. value is assigned X. value $+ X$. child, and we then X. child is assigned Y. sibchild. After the final stage of the second half, the desired values are stored in the N value fields. It is easy to verify that this algorithm requires $O(\log N)$ time on a plain hypercube or a hypercube-derived computer when $N = P$.

This algorithm for the scan problem reduces the number of active values by a factor of 2 during each stage of the first half. Although there are other $O(\log N)$ time scan algorithms that do not reduce the amount of data that is being processed,[221] this data reduction algorithm has the advantage that it can be used to obtain an optimal algorithm when $N > P$. In particular, if each processor simply simulates the behavior of a set of N/P consecutive processors in the above algorithm, an $O(N/P + \log P)$ time algorithm for the scan problem is obtained.

10.3.2 Segmented Scan

The other version of the parallel prefix problem that will be considered in this section is the segmented scan operation. The input to this operation is an array of N records, each of which has a data and a key field and an associative binary operator "$+$" with identity 0. For each of the key values, the set of records having that key value must occupy contiguous array locations. The segmented scan operation consists of performing a separate scan operation on each of the sets of records with matching key values. The segmented scan operation is useful because it allows a scan operation to be applied to many data sets in parallel.

Schwartz has shown that the segmented scan operation can be implemented with a single regular scan operation.[221] Specifically, define the binary operator "$*$" that operates on data and key pairs as follows. Let $(d1, k1)$ and $(d2, k2)$ be pairs of data and key values, let $(d1, k1) * (d2, k2)$ be $(d1 + d2, k1)$, if $k1 = k2$, and let $(d1, k1) * (d2, k2)$ be $(d2, k2)$ otherwise. A regular scan operation may simply be performed using the operator $*$ in order to implement the segmented scan operation.

10.3.3 Examples of Scan Operations

A few basic operations that can be implemented with scans will now be examined. The Rank operation was first introduced by Schwartz.[221] Suppose a subset of PEs holds a mark. The Rank operation consists of assigning the value i to the i-th marked PE. The Rank operation can be implemented by performing a single scan where the marked PEs are assigned the value 1, the unmarked PEs are assigned the value 0, and the binary operator is addition.

Another important use of scans is the broadcast operation.[221,251] Broadcast is also a special case of the parallel prefix problem, where the lists are composed of consecutive PEs. These lists are identified by a leader or header PE. The input to the broadcast operation is an array of N elements with a certain set of the elements designated as "leaders." These leaders partition the array into groups, with each group consisting of a leader and all of the successive locations up to, but not including, the next leader. The broadcast operation transmits the value of each leader to all of the locations in its group. The broadcast operation is easily implemented with a segmented scan.

Another use of the scan operation is the calculation of the maximum value in an array. In fact, it is straightforward to define the binary operator so that the value and the location of a maximum are found.

10.4 Monotonic Permutations

An important routing problem consists of implementing partial permutations. The input to the partial permutation problem is an array of N records, each of which has a pointer field (which may be null) and a data field. No two non-null pointers are allowed to have the same value. The problem is to send each data item to the array location pointed to by its associated pointer. Data items with null pointers do not have to be sent.

Algorithms for routing partial permutations will be considered in depth in Section 10.6. In this section, the focus will be on a restricted class of partial permutations, namely monotonic permutations. In a monotonic permutation, the non-null pointer fields are required to form a strictly increasing sequence. That is, if $i < j$ and neither pointer(i) nor pointer(j) is null, then pointer (i) < pointer (j). Although this restriction might appear very limiting, it turns out that the monotonic permutations are important subroutines in other more general operations, including general pointer operations (see Section 10.8). It will be shown that a monotonic permutation can be implemented in $O(\log N)$ time on a plain hypercube or a hypercube-derived computer with $P = N$ processors.[166]

Before solving the monotonic permutation problem, consider how a single data item can be routed to an arbitrary destination. Let X be the processor originally holding the item, let Z be the processor to which it will be sent, and let $p = \log P$. One simple algorithm examines the bits in the binary representations of X and Z in order from least to most significant. For each bit position i, if $X_{(i)} = Z_{(i)}$, then no routing is performed. However, if $X_{(i)} \neq Z_{(i)}$, then the data item is moved from its current location L to location $L^{(i)}$. Thus, before bit position i is examined, the item is in location $(X_{(p-1)}, X_{(p-2)}, \ldots, X_{(i)}, Z_{(i-1)}, Z_{(i-2)}, \ldots, Z_{(0)})$, and after bit position i is examined, it is in location $(X_{(p-1)}, X_{(p-2)}, \ldots, X_{(i+1)}, Z_{(i)}, Z_{(i-1)}, \ldots, Z_{(0)})$. This class ascend algorithm will move the item from location X to location Z, so the routing of a single data item can be performed in $O(\log N)$ time on a plain hypercube or a hypercube-derived computer. This simple routing algorithm will be called ascend routing. Of course, the routing could also be performed by examining the bit positions in the opposite order; the resulting class descend algorithm will be called descend routing.

It is tempting to use either ascend routing or descend routing to solve the monotonic permutation problem directly. However, this is not possible because data items could collide with one another. For example, consider two data items W and X that are being routed to locations Y and Z, respectively. If the ascend routing algorithm is used, there could be some i, $0 \leq i < p - 1$, for which $(W_{(p-1)}, W_{(p-2)}, \ldots, W_{(i+1)}, Y_{(i)}, Y_{(i-1)}, \ldots, Y_{(0)})$ is equal to $(X_{(p-1)}, X_{(p-2)}, \ldots, X_{(i+1)}, Z_{(i)}, Z_{(i-1)}, \ldots, Z_{(0)})$. Therefore, after performing the routing for bit position i, both data items will attempt to occupy the same location.

Because of this difficulty, the monotonic permutation problem will have to be decomposed into simpler subproblems that can be solved with ascend or descend routing. Specifically, instead of routing the active records directly to their destinations, an intermediate destination will be assigned to each active record. Each active record will be routed first to its intermediate destination and then to its final destination. Thus, the monotonic permutation algorithm consists of three subroutines. The first subroutine, called *rank*, assigns the intermediate destinations to the active records. The second subroutine, called *concentrate*, routes the active records to their intermediate destinations. The third subroutine, called *distribute*, routes the active records from their intermediate destinations to their final destinations. The resulting algorithm runs in $O(\log N)$ time and is quite simple and practical.

The rank subroutine (see Section 10.3.3) is used to determine, for each active record, the number of active records that precede it. That is, it assigns the value $i - 1$ to the i-th active record. The results of the rank operation are used as the intermediate destinations for the active records. It has already been shown that the rank operation can be performed in $O(\log N)$ time.

The concentrate operation[166] routes the active records to their intermediate destinations. Thus, a concentrate can be viewed as a monotonic permutation in which the i-th active record points to record $i - 1$. After performing a concentrate, the k active records have been copied to the first k positions of the array, without changing their relative order. Nassimi and Sahni have shown that the concentrate operation can be implemented without any collisions by using ascend routing.[166] To see this, assume for the sake of contradiction that a collision does occur. Then, there must be two active records W and X, which collide after performing the routing for some bit i. Let Y be the intermediate destination of W, let Z be the intermediate destination of X, and assume, without loss of generality, that $W < X$. Because W and X collide after performing the routing for bit i, $(W_{(p-1)}, W_{(p-2)}, \ldots, W_{(i+1)}, Y_{(i)}, Y_{(i-1)}, \ldots, Y_{(0)})$ is equal to $(X_{(p-1)}, X_{(p-2)}, \ldots, X_{(i+1)}, Z_{(i)}, Z_{(i-1)}, \ldots, Z_{(0)})$. Because $Y_{(j)} = Z_{(j)}$ for all j, $0 \leq j \leq i$,

$$Z - Y \geq 2i + 1,$$

which implies that

$$X - W \geq 2i + 1,$$

which implies that

$$W_{(j)} = X_{(j)}$$

for some j, $i + 1 \leq j \leq p - 1$, which is a contradiction.

Finally, the distribute operation[166] routes the active records from their intermediate destinations to their final destinations. Thus, a distribute can be viewed as a monotonic permutation in which the active records all precede the inactive records. The distribute operation can be implemented without any collisions by using descend routing.[166] The fact that there are no collisions follows from the observation that the distribute operation is the inverse of the concentrate operation, and it has been shown that the concentrate operation can be performed without collisions by using ascend routing.

10.5 Simulating Multiple Machines

A common criticism of processor-based parallel computers is that they are rigid and cannot operate on several independent groups of data simultaneously. This criticism is unfounded. It is possible to partition the P PEs into smaller groups of consecutive processors and to have each group perform a computation on an independent set of data. This operation is called multiple machine simulation. Suppose that each group contains K consecutive PEs, where K is a power of 2, and assume that the first group starts in PE 0. Then, every group can perform an ascend or descend algorithm (see Chapter 9) with $O(\log K)$ time for communication. This property is obvious for a hypercube computer because each block of PEs constitutes a hypercube of dimension $\log K$.

Interestingly, the same result holds for the constant degree networks discussed in Chapter 9, because the ascend or descend algorithm within groups can be considered to be a bit-block algorithm running on the entire machine (see Section 9.6). It is interesting to notice that on the constant degree architectures, the data from a single group are sent to processors outside of the group during the algorithm. For example, on an SE computer, the shuffle and unshuffle operations move data items between the groups of processors. As a result, it is essential that the machine is operating in an SIMD mode, with the same calculation being performed on each group. In contrast, the hypercube can be partitioned into separate subcubes that can perform hypercube computations independently, so an MIMD hypercube could be partitioned and used by many users at a single time. Of course, multiple users could be accommodated on the constant degree networks by using time-sharing.

Even if the group sizes are not identical and are not powers of 2, ascend and descend algorithms within groups can be implemented efficiently on plain hypercubes or on hypercube-derived computers (an ascend or descend algorithm can be applied to an array with a length that is not a power of 2 by padding it with null items). In particular, in $O(\log P)$ time each group of size K can be moved to a subcube with at least $K/4$ processors. The ascend or descend algorithms can then be performed within these subcubes. The algorithm for moving each group to its subcube is an interesting application of the communication primitives presented earlier. A segmented scan is first performed so that the last processor in each group knows the size of its group. The last processor in each group then determines the size and location of the largest subcube contained in the group. This subcube is guaranteed to be at least one-fourth as large as the group itself. Another segmented scan is then performed to broadcast the starting position of the group's subcube from the last processor in the group to the remaining processors in the group. Next, each processor adds its position within the group (obtained during the first segmented scan) to the subcube's starting position to obtain the destination for its data item. These data items are then sent to their destinations using a monotonic permutation on a $4P$ processor machine (which is being simulated by the P processor machine with a constant factor slowdown).

10.6 Partial Permutations

In Section 10.4, the partial permutation problem was defined. The input to this problem is an array of N records, each of which consists of a pointer field (that may be null) and a data field. No two non-null pointers are allowed to point to the same location. The problem is to send each data item that has a non-null pointer to the location given by its pointer. Two types of permutations will be considered, namely static and dynamic ones. In the static permutation problem, the permutation is known at compile time, and the compiler is allowed to perform time-consuming calculations in order to optimize the implementation of the permutation. In analyzing the time requirements of the static permutation problem, only the time spent actually performing the permutation is counted; the time that the compiler spends deciding how to perform the permutation is ignored. In the dynamic permutation problem, the permutation is only known when it is to be performed. As a result, the time spent deciding how to perform the permutation is counted in the analysis of the dynamic permutation problem.

10.6.1 Static Permutations

Static permutations can be used to solve some very common problems. For example, they can be used to simulate one interconnection topology with another. Static permutations can also be used to implement more general communication patterns, such as one-to-many mappings, provided that the communication pattern is known at compile time. These more general communication patterns will be discussed in Section 10.8.

There is a well-known algorithm for solving the static permutation problem in $O(\log N)$ time on hypercube or hypercube-derived computers with $P = N$ processors.[196,221,232] The algorithm is based on simulating a connecting network that is known as the Benes network,[20,260] therefore, it will be called the Benes routing algorithm.

The Benes routing algorithm is very similar to the algorithm for performing monotonic permutations that was presented in Section 10.4. Recall that the monotonic permutation problem cannot be solved without collisions by performing a single ascend or descend route. However, any monotonic permutation can be performed by first using an ascend route to send each item to an intermediate destination and then using a descend route to send each item to its final destination. The Benes routing algorithm has an identical structure; each item is first routed to an intermediate destination by using an ascend route and then routed to its final destination by using a descend route. The only difference between the monotonic permutation algorithm and the Benes routing algorithm is in the definition of the intermediate destinations. In the monotonic permutation algorithm, the definition of the intermediate destinations was very simple, namely the i-th active record has an intermediate destination of $i - 1$. In the Benes routing algorithm, the definition of the intermediate destinations is more complex. In this subsection, the correctness of the Benes routing algorithm (that is, that a set of suitable intermediate destinations exists) will be proven, and in the next subsection, an algorithm for finding the desired intermediate destinations will be given. For simplicity, it will be assumed that there are no null pointers, but the existence of null pointers does not affect the correctness of the algorithm.

Let $P = N = 2^n$. The proof of correctness of the Benes routing algorithm is by induction on n. The base case is $n = 1$. When $n = 1$, there are only two items to route. This case is trivially solved by having the intermediate destinations equal the final destinations.

The induction hypothesis is that the Benes routing algorithm works for any $n < k$. It will be shown that the induction hypothesis implies that the algorithm works for $n = k$. It will also be shown how the least significant bit of the intermediate destinations can be calculated so as to avoid collisions. The remaining bits of the intermediate destinations will then be set by using the induction hypothesis. Consider any two data items X and X', where X will be routed to location Z via the intermediate destination Y, and X' will be routed to location Z' via the intermediate destination Y'. In order to avoid a collision between these two items, it is required that

$$(X_{(n-1)}, X_{(n-2)}, \ldots, X_{(1)}, Y_{(0)}) \neq (X'_{(n-1)}, X'_{(n-2)}, \ldots, X'_{(1)}, Y'_{(0)})$$

and that

$$(Z_{(n-1)}, Z_{(n-2)}, \ldots, Z_{(1)}, Y_{(0)}) \neq (Z'_{(n-1)}, Z'_{(n-2)}, \ldots, Z'_{(1)}, Y'_{(0)}).$$

The items X and X' will be called a source pair if $X_{(i)} = X_{(i)'}$ for all i, $1 \leq i \leq n - 1$, and they will be called a destination pair if $Z_{(i)} = Z_{(i)'}$ for all i, $1 \leq i \leq n - 1$. Thus, in order to avoid a collision, $Y_{(0)}$ must not equal $Y_{(0)'}$ whenever X and X' are either a source or destination pair.

These requirements can always be satisfied. To see this, create the graph G that expresses these constraints. The vertices of G are numbered from 0 through $N - 1$, representing the N data items. There is an edge (called a source edge) between each pair of vertices that represents a source pair of data items, and there is an edge (called a destination edge) between each pair of vertices that represents a destination pair of data items. In order that no two vertices that are connected by an edge receive the same value, 0s and 1s must be assigned to the vertices. It is easy to see that each vertex has exactly one source edge and one destination edge incident to it. As a result, the edges in the graph form cycles of alternating source and destination edges, and each cycle is of even length. Therefore, it is possible to assign a 0 to every other vertex on a cycle and a 1 to the remaining vertices on the cycle, thus, satisfying the criteria.

Let the 0s and 1s assigned to the vertices of G be the values of the least significant bits of the intermediate locations. It is known that with these bits assigned to the intermediate locations, there can be no collisions following the first routing step or preceding the last routing step. Thus, all that remains is the setting of the other bits in the intermediate destinations so that there are no collisions during the remaining routing steps. However, the data items that are routed through even intermediate destinations will be in even locations during all of the remaining routing steps, and likewise for the data items that are routed through odd intermediate destinations. Therefore, the induction hypothesis guarantees that the $N/2$ data items with even intermediate destinations can be routed from location $(X_{(n-1)}, X_{(n-2)}, \ldots, X_{(1)}, Y_{(0)})$ to location $(Z_{(n-1)}, Z_{n-2}) \ldots Z_{(1)}, Y_{(0)})$, without collisions, and likewise for the data items with odd intermediate destinations. This completes the proof of correctness for the Benes routing algorithm.

It has been shown that the Benes routing algorithm performs static permutations in $O(\log N)$ time by routing each data item through some intermediate destination. However, it has not been shown how these intermediate destinations can be chosen efficiently. Although the time required to choose the intermediate destinations is not counted in the time analysis of the static permutation problem, it would still be favorable to calculate these destinations efficiently because they must be chosen by a compiler. How to choose the intermediate destinations using a hypercube or hypercube-derived computer will be considered.

In the proof of correctness, a graph G, was created that represented the constraints on the least significant bits of the intermediate destinations. In order to calculate the least significant bits of the intermediate destinations, 0s and 1s must alternately be assigned to the vertices in each of the cycles in G. One way to do this is to start by assigning a 0 to the smallest numbered vertex in each cycle. Nassimi and Sahni have shown how this assignment of 0s and 1s can be calculated using a hypercube computer.[171] Their algorithm will be reviewed here.

Let X be any data item and let X' and X'' be such that X and X' are a source pair and X' and X'' are a destination pair. In the graph G, there is a source edge connecting X and X' and there is a destination edge connecting X' and X''. Therefore, X and X'' must receive the same value. In Nassimi and Sahni's algorithm, each data item X creates a pointer to its corresponding item X''. These pointers create circular-linked lists consisting of every other vertex in the cycles in graph G. Nassimi and Sahni find the smallest numbered vertex in each of these circular-linked lists, and they assign 0s to the vertices in the linked lists that have an even smallest member and they assign 1s to the vertices in the linked lists that have an odd smallest member. It is easy to verify that this assignment of 0s and 1s corresponds to assigning a 0 to the smallest numbered vertex in each cycle of G and alternately assigning 1s and 0s to the remaining vertices in the cycle.

The problem of finding the smallest numbered vertex in each linked list is known as the list reduction problem, which is a special case of the data-dependent parallel prefix problem. Nassimi and Sahni solve the list reduction problem by using a routine that requires $O(\log^3 N)$ time on a hypercube computer. Thus, the least significant bit of the intermediate destinations is calculated in $O(\log^3 N)$ time. The remaining bits of the intermediate destinations are calculated recursively, therefore, their entire algorithm for calculating the intermediate destinations requires $O(\log^4 N)$ time. In Section 10.10, it will be shown how to solve the list reduction problem in $O(\log^2 N \log\log N)$ time.[51] By using this list reduction algorithm, an $O(\log^3 N \log\log N)$ time algorithm for calculating the intermediate destinations using a hypercube or hypercube-derived computer will be obtained.

10.6.2 Dynamic Permutations

Dynamic permutations arise in many algorithms. For example, they can be used to communicate between processors in a data-dependent manner, provided that no two processors attempt to send data to the same processor.

Two basic approaches have been used to solve the dynamic permutation problem on hypercube and hypercube-derived computers. First, the dynamic permutation problem has been treated as being a special case of the sorting problem. Algorithms for sorting on hypercubes will be presented in Section 10.7. Second, randomized algorithms with good expected case behavior have been developed. Some of these randomized algorithms will be reviewed here.

One of the simplest randomized algorithms for dynamic permutations was given by Valiant and Brebner.[257] Their algorithm is essentially the same as the monotonic permutation and Benes routing algorithms, except that the intermediate destinations are chosen at random. That is, each data item first chooses an intermediate destination randomly and independently. Then, the data items are routed to their intermediate destinations using ascend routing and from their intermediate destinations to their final destinations using descend routing (or ascend routing; it makes no difference). Of course, it is possible that there will be collisions when attempting to perform these routes. As a result, there is a queue associated with each outgoing communication link. When more than one data item attempts to traverse a given link at a given time, one of them succeeds and the others are placed in the queue associated with the link. Thus, the data items traverse the paths specified by the ascend or descend routing algorithms, but they may be delayed occasionally by other data items.

Valiant and Brebner have shown that this simple routing algorithm solves the dynamic permutation problem in $O(\log N)$ time on a hypercube with strong communication (all $\log N$ wires leaving a processor are used simultaneously) with overwhelming probability. It is important to note that the expected running time of their algorithm is independent of the permutation that is being routed. This is because the use of random intermediate destinations makes all permutations look the same. The fact that all permutations have the same performance is convenient, because it allows simulations to be performed for one permutation (say the identity permutation) and the results to be applied to all permutations.

The queues in Valiant and Brebner's algorithm are never larger than $O(\log N)$ (with overwhelming probability). When more than one data item attempts to leave a processor along a given link, the rule that specifies which data item succeeds in leaving is called the queuing discipline. Any queuing discipline can be used in Valiant and Brebner's algorithm without affecting the above time bounds. In particular, a simple first-in-first-out (FIFO) queuing discipline can be used.

The process of sending the items to random intermediate destinations typically increases the distance that the packets travel. For example, if a random permutation is being implemented, then the average distance that a data item travels will be doubled. As a result, it is tempting to eliminate the use of intermediate destinations and just use ascend routing, with queues, to perform the permutation. In fact, if the permutation to be routed is itself random, then this can be done, while still having the probabilistic $O(\log N)$ time bound. This is because the whole purpose of the intermediate destinations is to make any permutation look like a random permutation.

However, if the permutation to be routed is not random, the use of the random intermediate destinations is essential. A routing algorithm is called oblivious if the route that each data item takes is independent of the destinations of the other data items. Oblivious routing algorithms can be further classified as being deterministic, in which the route that a data item takes is a function of its source and destination, or randomized, in which the route that a data item takes is a function of its source, its destination, and some random bits. Using this classification, Valiant and Brebner's routing algorithm is randomized and oblivious. Kaklamanis, Krizanc, and Tsantilas have proven that any deterministic oblivious routing algorithm on a degree d interconnection network requires time proportional to $N^{1/2}/d$ for some permutation.[123] Thus, just using ascend routing without intermediate destinations works in $O(\log N)$ time for almost all permutations, but it takes time proportional to $N^{1/2}/\log N$ for at least one permutation.

Still, because almost all permutations can be routed quickly in this manner, it might be hoped that in practice the few bad permutations will never be encountered and the routing to intermediate destinations may be skipped. Unfortunately, this is not the case. Although not many permutations are bad, it turns out that many of the commonly used permutations are bad. For example, let $n = \log N$ and let $m = n/2$. Then, performing a matrix transpose sends the item in processor $(A_{n-1}, A_{n-2}, \ldots, A_0)$ to processor $(A_{m-1}, A_{m-2}, \ldots, A_0, A_{n-1}, A_{n-2}, \ldots, A_m)$. When an ascend routing strategy is used, all $N^{1/2}$ data items that begin in processors of the form $(A_{n-1}, A_{n-2}, \ldots, A_m, *, \ldots, *)$

are routed through processor $(A_{m-1}, A_{m-2}, \ldots, A_0, A_{m-1}, A_{m-2}, \ldots, A_0)$. Because this processor can send at most log N items at a time, the transpose requires time proportional to $N^{1/2}/\log N$.

A difficulty with Valiant and Brebner's routing algorithm is the fact that it runs only on a network with a log N degree. Upfal overcame this limitation by creating a routing algorithm that implements any given permutation on a BF computer in $O(\log N)$ time with overwhelming probability.[252] Upfal's algorithm is similar to Valiant and Brebner's algorithm. Specifically, consider a data item that is being routed from row R1 and column C1 of the BF to row R2 and column C2. This item is first routed to a random row in column C1, then to a random row in column C2, and finally to the destination. The main difference in Upfal's algorithm is the queuing discipline. While simple FIFO queues could be used in Valiant and Brebner's algorithm, Upfal's algorithm requires priority queues that select the data item that has gone the shortest distance.

A number of other randomized routing algorithms have been developed. Aleliunas created a randomized scheme for routing on the SE in $O(\log N)$ expected time.[7] Pippenger designed a routing algorithm for the BF that implements any permutation in $O(\log N)$ expected time with constant size queues.[184] Pippenger's algorithm is quite complex and has a large constant of proportionality in its running time. Finally, Ranade created a simple BF routing algorithm that terminates in $O(\log N)$ time with overwhelming probability and uses only a constant number of words of memory per processor.[201] Furthermore, Ranade's scheme can perform many-to-one mappings assuming that the data items with a common destination can be merged. Ranade's algorithm will be examined in Section 10.8.

10.7 Sorting

A great deal of research has been devoted to developing efficient parallel sorting algorithms.[6,27] Parallel sorting algorithms have been created for a variety of models including parallel comparison trees,[9,255] sorting networks,[5,16,52,132,195] shared memory computers,[25,44,108,197] and distributed memory computers, such as hypercubes and meshes. Sorting algorithms for hypercube and hypercube-derived computers are important for two reasons. First, sorting is an important operation in sequential computers and also plays a key role in parallel algorithms. Second, sorting is fundamental to several algorithms for performing pointer-based communication (see Section 10.8). In this section, some of the sorting algorithms that have been developed for hypercube and hypercube-derived computers will be reviewed.

10.7.1 Bitonic Sorting

One of the earliest and most important parallel sorting algorithms is Batcher's bitonic sort.[16,232] It has already been shown in Chapter 5 that the bitonic sort can be used to obtain an $O(N^{1/2})$ time sorting algorithm for mesh connected computers with $P = N$ processors. When it is implemented on a plain hypercube or a hypercube-derived computer, the bitonic sort runs in $O(\log^2 N)$ time if $N = P$.

The bitonic sorting algorithm is a merge sort that merges pairs of sorted lists each containing 2^i items, where i goes from 0 through $\log N - 1$. Batcher's bitonic merge algorithm[16] is used to perform the merges.

A sequence is bitonic if it consists of a monotonically increasing sequence followed by a monotonically decreasing sequence or if it can be rotated cyclically to obtain a monotonically increasing sequence followed by a monotonically decreasing one. Batcher's bitonic merge algorithm sorts a bitonic sequence of length $N = 2^n$ by performing compare-exchange operations on items in locations that differ in bit positions $n - 1, n - 2, \ldots, 0$. Each compare-exchange operation compares two items and exchanges them if they are out of order.

Batcher uses the bitonic merge algorithm to merge a pair of sorted sequences by first concatenating the sorted sequences with one being sorted in ascending order and the other being sorted in descending order. The concatenated sequences form a bitonic sequence that can be sorted with the bitonic merge algorithm. Thus, in each phase of the bitonic sorting algorithm, one-half of the bitonic merges produce sequences that are sorted in ascending order and the other half produce sequences that are sorted in descending order. The ascending and descending sequences alternate so that pairs of adjacent sequences can be used as input for the next phase of bitonic merges.

The bitonic merge is a class descend algorithm. As a result, a bitonic merge of a N item list can be implemented in $O(\log N)$ time on a plain hypercube computer when $N = P$. Because the bitonic sort consists of $\log N$ bitonic merges, the bitonic sort requires $O(\log^2 N)$ time on a plain hypercube computer with $P = N$ processors.

The correctness of the bitonic merge algorithm can be proven as follows. The first step consists of comparing items that are 2^{i-1} locations apart and exchanging them if they are out of order. When this operation is applied to a bitonic sequence, it can be guaranteed that the result has two properties. First, the smallest 2^{i-1} items must be in the first 2^{i-1} locations and the largest 2^{i-1} items must be in the last 2^{i-1} locations. Second, the first 2^{i-1} items must form a bitonic sequence and the last 2^{i-1} items must form a bitonic sequence.

To see why these two properties hold, consider the original bitonic sequence of length 2^i. The largest 2^{i-1} items in this sequence must be located in a set of 2^{i-1} consecutive locations (if the locations are ordered cyclically), and they must form a bitonic sequence of length 2^{i-1}. Thus, when items that are 2^{i-1} locations apart are compared, one item in each pair will be in the set of 2^{i-1} largest items and the other will not. As a result, the largest 2^{i-1} items will be placed in the last 2^{i-1} locations. Also, the relative order of these largest 2^{i-1} items will not be changed, except by cyclically rotating them, so the resulting sequence of length 2^{i-1} will be bitonic. An analogous argument proves that the smallest 2^{i-1} items also form a bitonic sequence.

Thus, the first stage of a bitonic merge divides the bitonic sequence into two separate bitonic sequences, one consisting of the smaller items and the other of the larger items. The remainder of the bitonic merge algorithm consists of performing bitonic merges on these two subsequences in parallel. As a result, the correctness of the bitonic merge can be proven inductively. The base case consists of merging two sequences each of length 1, which is easily shown to be correct.

The bitonic sorting algorithm is a simple and practical algorithm. For example, when it is implemented on a plain hypercube computer, it requires only $(\log N)(\log N + 1)/2$ stages, each of which consists of a compare and exchange operation between connected processors. Thus, although its $O(\log^2 N)$ complexity is not optimal, the small constant of proportionality in its running time makes it very attractive in practice. In the following two subsections, algorithms for sorting when the number of data items does not equal the number of processors will be examined. Then, the focus will return to the problem of sorting on hypercube computers when $N = P$, and an algorithm that is asymptotically more efficient than the bitonic sort will be shown.

10.7.2 Sorting with $N > P$

In practice, it is very common for the number of data items that must be sorted to be greater than the number of processors that are available. Of course, one way to solve this problem is to use an algorithm for the case $N = P$ and to simulate a machine with N processors (see Section 10.1). When this approach is used with the bitonic sort, an $O((N/P)\log^2 N))$ time algorithm is obtained. However, more efficient algorithms have been designed that take advantage of the fact that $N > P$.

One of the first such algorithms was presented by Baudet and Stevenson.[18] Their algorithm is an application of a general technique developed by Knuth.[132] Recall that in the bitonic sort, pairs of items are compared, and they are exchanged if they are out of order. This process of comparing and conditionally exchanging a pair of items is called a compare-exchange operation. Knuth's technique converts any algorithm for sorting P items that is based on compare-exchange operations into an algorithm for sorting $N > P$ items. First, each processor sorts its N/P items by using a sequential sorting algorithm. Then, the algorithm for sorting P items is implemented, where each compare-exchange operation is replaced by a merge-split operation. A merge-split operation first merges two sorted lists, each of length N/P, and then splits the resulting list at the median. By applying this technique to the bitonic sort, Baudet and Stevenson obtained an $O((N/P)\log(N/P) + (N/P)\log^2 P))$ time sorting algorithm. A similar algorithm was presented by Johnsson.[119] Johnsson's algorithm has the same asymptotic complexity as that of Baudet and Stevenson.

An algorithm for a special case of the sorting problem was given by Gottlieb and Kruskal.[95] They presented a shuffle-exchange algorithm for the permutation problem, where the N numbers to be sorted are in the range 1 through N and where each number appears once. Their algorithm requires $O(P^{9/2} + (N/P)\log P)$ time.

More recently, Aggarwal and Huang created a sorting algorithm for the case $N > P$ that runs in $O((N/P)\log N[\log N/\log(N/P)]^{\alpha})$ time, where $\alpha = (3 - \log 3)/(\log 3 - 1)$ or approximately 2.419.[1] Also, Cypher and Sanz created an algorithm called *cubesort* that sorts in $O((N/P)\log^2 N/\log(N/P))$ time provided $\log^{\beta} N \leq N/P \leq N^{\beta}$ for some positive integer β.[51,56-58] The above time bounds hold for both plain hypercube computers as well as hypercube-derived computers. Note that whenever $N = P^{1+\varepsilon}$ for some positive constant ε, both Aggarwal and Huang's algorithm and cubesort are optimal with respect to sequential comparison sorting. However, as N becomes closer to P, cubesort outperforms Aggarwal and Huang's algorithm. For example, if $N = P \log P$, cubesort requires $O((\log^3 P)/\log\log P)$ time, and Aggarwal and Huang's algorithm requires approximately $O(\log^{4.419} P)$ time.

Cubesort has a very simple structure. It can be viewed as consisting of separate stages, which will be called sort-permute stages, In each sort-permute stage, every processor sorts the N/P items that it holds, and then the data items are redistributed between the processors according to a fixed permutation (one that is known at compile time). Only a small number of different fixed permutations are needed. Also, the permutations that are required are defined in terms of shifting the binary representations of the addresses, so they can be implemented very efficiently on plain hypercube and hypercube-derived computers. When $N = P^{1+\varepsilon}$ for some positive constant epsilon, only a constant number of sort-permute stages are required. In general, cubesort requires $O((\log^2 N)/[\log^2 (N/P)])$ sort-permute stages.

It is interesting to notice that a number of other parallel sorting algorithms have a similar structure. That is, they can all be viewed as breaking the problem of sorting N items into successive stages of partitioning the N items into G groups of size N/G and sorting within the groups. One such algorithm is *shearsort*.[215] Shearsort sorts N items by performing $O(\log N)$ stages, where each stage sorts groups of $N^{1/2}$ elements. Another algorithm is *revsort*.[218] Revsort also sorts groups of $N^{1/2}$ items, but it requires only $O(\log\log N)$ stages. A still more efficient algorithm is *columnsort*.[147] Columnsort sorts N items by performing a constant number of stages of sorting groups with approximately $N^{2/3}$ items. Columnsort can be called recursively to handle smaller group sizes. In fact, this is the basis of Aggarwal and Huang's sorting algorithm.[1]

Another efficient sorting algorithm for the case $N > P$ is Plaxton's *smoothsort*.[187,188] Smoothsort has a structure somewhat similar to *quicksort*. However, rather than selecting a single value to partition the items into two sets, a number of evenly spaced values are used to partition the items into multiple sets. The items in each set are sent to a subcube devoted to that set, and these subcubes are then sorted recursively. When the items are first routed to their appropriate subcubes, some processors may have more items than others. In order to smooth out the load before performing the recursive sort, a load-balancing operation is performed (both before and after sending the items to their subcubes). This load balancing requires that each processor communicate with only a single neighbor at a time, but it works best if different processors can communicate across different dimensions of the hypercube at the same time. As a result, smoothsort has a better running time on a hypercube with independent communication than on a plain hypercube.

Let $X = \log^{1.5} P \log\log P$. When $N \le PX$, smoothsort runs on a hypercube with weak independent communication in $O(\log(N/P)\log^3 P)$ time, and when $N > PX$, smoothsort runs on a hypercube with weak independent communication in $O((N/P)\log^{1.5} P/\log^{0.5} (N/PX) + \log(N/P)\log^3 P)$ time. Plaxton also created an algorithm based on smoothsort that runs on a plain hypercube or a hypercube-derived computer. This algorithm has a running time of $O((N/P)(\log^2 P)/\log(N/P))$. This matches the running cubesort's running time on these models, plus it has two advantages. First, it can be used for any value of $N \ge P$. Second, it has a smaller constant of proportionality in its running time, thus, making it competitive with bitonic sort for realistic values of N and P.

Finally, Section 10.7.4 will show a nonconstructive algorithm for sorting $N = P$ items on a plain hypercube or a hypercube related computer in $O(\log N \log\log N)$ time. By simulating a larger hypercube, this yields an $O((N/P)\log N \log\log N)$ time sorting algorithm when $N > P$. A similar constructive algorithm will be shown that yields an $O((N/P)\log N \log\log^2 N)$ sorting algorithm when $N > P$. The constants in these algorithms are large, so they are probably not the best choice in practice.

10.7.3 Sorting with $N > P$

Although it is not usual in practice to have more processors than items to sort, the problem of sorting when $N < P$ is important because it is used as a subroutine in many other algorithms.[213] When $N < P$, an enumeration sort created by Nassimi and Sahni[170] can be used. Their algorithm, which will be called the sparse enumeration sort, is an implementation of an EREW PRAM sorting algorithm developed by Preparata.[197] Let $G = P/N$. The sparse enumeration sort requires $O(\log N \log P/\log G)$ time on a plain hypercube or a hypercube-derived computer.

The sparse enumeration sort is a merge sort that repeatedly merges sets of G sorted lists. Each merge of G lists consists of three steps. First, for each item i and list j, the number of items in j that are smaller than i is calculated. Call this value $count(i, j)$. Second, each item i determines its destination, $dest(i)$, which is the total number of items in the G lists that are less than i. The destination for item i is calculated by adding together the values $count(i, j)$ for all lists j. Third, each item is moved to its destination.

The first step is implemented by performing bitonic merges. Assume that each of the G sorted lists contains N/G items. The processors are divided into G^2 groups of N/G consecutive processors. The k-th group of processors performs a bitonic merge of the lists x and y where $x = k$ mod G and $y =$ floor(k/G). Following the merge of lists x and y, each item i in list x can calculate count(i, y) by subtracting its position in list x from its position in the list formed by merging lists x and y. The second and third steps are implemented with class ascend and descend algorithms.

Finally, Section 10.7.4 will show a nonconstructive algorithm for sorting $N = P$ items on a plain hypercube or a hypercube related computer in $O(\log N \log\log N)$ time. This same algorithm can of course be used when $N < P$. The resulting algorithm gives the best known time bounds when $N \leq P \leq N^{1+1/\log\log N}$, in which case it requires $O(\log N \log\log N)$ time.

10.7.4 Sorting with $N = P$

Earlier it was shown that the bitonic sort requires $O(\log^2 N)$ time to sort on a plain hypercube or a hypercube-related computer when $N = P$. The only lower bound that is known for this problem is that any hypercube sorting algorithm will have to take time proportional to log N, the diameter of the network. If an $O(\log N)$ time hypercube sorting algorithm for the case $N = P$ could be developed, it would represent an optimal speed-up over sequential comparison sorting. Although no hypercube sorting algorithm with a worst case $O(\log N)$ time performance has been developed, several algorithms that are asymptotically more efficient than the bitonic sort have been created.

Reif and Valiant created a randomized sorting algorithm that runs in $O(\log N)$ time with overwhelming probability on the CCC.[204] Because of the relationship between the CCC and the other hypercube-derived computers,[220] Reif and Valiant's algorithm has the same complexity on any hypercube-derived computer. Their algorithm uses randomized routing techniques similar to those presented in Section 10.8. The algorithm is quite complicated and the constant of proportionality in its running time makes it unlikely to be practical.

Cypher and Plaxton have created a deterministic sorting algorithm, called *sharesort*, that runs in $O(\log N \log\log N)$ time on a plain hypercube or a hypercube-derived computer when $N = P$.[54,55] Sharesort is nonconstructive; that is, it requires the use of information, specifically, routing tables, which are guaranteed to exist but which take an exponential amount of time to create. A constructive version of sharesort has also been developed that runs in $O(\log N \log\log^2 N)$ time on the same type of computers.[54] Sharesort has a complex structure and a large constant of proportionality in its running time, so it is surely slower than the bitonic sort for practical values of N.

Sharesort makes extensive use of the communication routines presented in this chapter. In fact, the constructive version is composed entirely of scan operations (Section 10.3), monotonic permutations (Section 10.4), static per-

mutations (Section 10.6), bitonic merges (Section 10.7.1), and sparse enumeration sorts (Section 10.7.3). The nonconstructive version uses these same
routines, plus a deterministic routing algorithm based on the randomized
routing algorithm of Valiant and Brebner (Section 10.8).

There is some flexibility in the definition of sharesort, as several of the
parameters (such as the sizes of the recursive calls) can be varied without
changing the overall complexity. A simple version will be sketched here. All
of the data items will be assumed to be distinct, as it is easy to break ties by
concatenating the item's original position to its key. Sharesort sorts an array
of N items by dividing it into $N^{1/2}$ lists of length $N^{1/2}$ each and sorting these
lists recursively and in parallel. These $N^{1/2}$ sorted lists are then merged to
form a single sorted list of length N. This merging procedure, which is called
squaremerge, requires $O(\log N \log\log N)$ time in the nonconstructive version
and $O(\log N \log\log^2 N)$ time in the constructive version.

Squaremerge merges the $N^{1/2}$ sorted lists by using a bucket sort approach. The data items are assigned to $N^{1/3}$ buckets of size $N^{2/3}$ each,
where all of the items in any bucket i are greater than all of the items
in bucket $i - 1$. Each bucket i, $0 \le i < N^{2/3}$, is allocated processors $iN^{2/3}$
through $(i + 1)N^{2/3} - 1$. The data items are then routed to the processors in
their bucket. At this point, items in separate buckets are correctly ordered,
but within buckets, items can be out of order. The final step is to complete the
sort within the buckets. Thus, squaremerge has three parts: (1) assign items to
buckets, (2) route items to buckets, and (3) sort within buckets. How these
three parts are accomplished will now be examined.

It is common in a bucket sort to be able to use the value of a data item to
determine to which bucket it belongs. However, in sharesort, there are no
assumptions about the values of the data items, and the buckets must be
exactly the same size. As a result, the value of the smallest item in each
bucket must first be determined. More formally, let the rank of an item be the
number of other items that are less than it. Then, the items with ranks of the
form $iN^{2/3}$, for any integer i, $0 \le i < N^{1/3}$, will be the smallest items in their
respective buckets. These will be called $N^{1/3}$ items splitters. Once the splitters
have been calculated, a sorted list of the splitters can be merged with each
sorted list of $N^{1/2}$ items and a scan operation can be performed to calculate
the bucket to which each item belongs.

The splitters are calculated by taking samples from the $N^{1/2}$ sorted lists.
Specifically, every $N^{1/12}$-th item is taken from each of the sorted lists, thus,
creating $N^{11/12}$-th samples. These samples are then sorted with the sparse
enumeration sort. This sorted list of samples gives a great deal of information about the desired splitters. Although the sorted samples do not provide
the exact values of the splitters, they do eliminate all but $O(N^{7/12})$ items
from consideration as being the i-th splitter for any i. Because $N^{1/3}$ different
splitters are being looked for, at most $O(N^{11/12})$ items have a possibility
of being one of the desired splitters. These $O(N^{11/12})$ items are sorted
with the sparse enumeration sort to determine which $N^{1/3}$ of them are the

desired splitters. Thus, the entire splitter finding task requires only $O(\log N)$ time.

The next task is routing the data items to their buckets. Consider the $N^{1/2}$ items in any of the sorted lists. These items will go to $N^{1/3}$ different buckets, and the items that are destined for the same bucket form a block of consecutive items (because the list is sorted). These blocks will contain an average of $N^{1/6}$ items each, although it will be common for some blocks to be longer than others. In order to simplify the description, assume that every such block is exactly $N^{1/6}$ long. Later, how variable-sized blocks can be handled will be explained.

The problem of routing the blocks of length $N^{1/6}$ to their buckets is best described by viewing the data as forming an $N^{5/6}$ by $N^{1/6}$ array, where each row is a block of items destined for the same bucket. The problem of routing the blocks to the buckets can be viewed as a sorting problem in which the sort key is the bucket number. Because all of the items in a block share the same key value, this routine is called shared key sorting. Note that the shared key sorting problem can be solved by reordering the rows of the $N^{5/6}$ by $N^{1/6}$ array.

The first step in the shared key sorting algorithm is to take the first item in each row and sort these $N^{5/6}$ items with the sparse enumeration sort. This tells to which row each row must be sent. At this point, all that is necessary is to figure out how to route the blocks to the correct rows. Each item will be routed to the correct row without changing the column that it is in, therefore, this routing problem can be viewed as being a permutation of the items in each column, with the same permutation being applied in all of the columns in parallel. The key observation is that although all N data items must be permuted, only one type of permutation of $N^{5/6}$ is being used. The algorithm for performing this permutation has two halves. In the first half, a plan is developed for how to implement the permutation efficiently. In the second half, this plan is implemented. In the second half, there are N processors available for permuting N items, so the processors and data are balanced. However, in the first half, N processors are available for developing a plan for how to permute only $N^{5/6}$ items. The constructive and nonconstructive algorithms use different techniques to implement the shared key sort, but they both obtain their efficiency from this imbalance between the number of processors available during the planning half of the algorithm (N) and the number of items being permuted ($N^{5/6}$). The constructive algorithm solves the shared key sorting problem in $O(\log N \log\log N)$ time, while the nonconstructive algorithm solves it in $O(\log N)$ time.

The third and final part of the squaremerge algorithm consists of completing the sort within the buckets. Because each block is assumed to be exactly $N^{1/6}$ long, each bucket consists of $N^{1/2}$ blocks of length $N^{1/6}$, where the items in any one block appear in sorted order. The problem is to merge these sorted blocks to obtain a single sorted list of $N^{2/3}$ items. This is accomplished by using two recursive calls to squaremerge. First, sets of $N^{1/6}$ blocks, each of length $N^{1/6}$, are merged to obtain sorted lists of length $N^{1/3}$. Next, all $N^{1/3}$ of these sorted lists of length $N^{1/3}$ are merged to obtain a sorted list of length $N^{2/3}$. At this point, the items in each bucket are in sorted order, and the squaremerge has been completed.

This description completes the outline of sharesort, except that all of the blocks have been assumed to be exactly $N^{1/6}$ long. The above algorithm must be adapted slightly to accommodate variable length blocks. Specifically, within each sorted list of $N^{1/2}$ items, some of the blocks may be longer than $N^{1/6}$ and some may be shorter. First, each of the longer ones are partitioned into separate blocks of length $N^{1/6}$ (and possibly, one block that is shorter than $N^{1/6}$). At this point, no block is too long, but some of them may be too short. Next, all of the short blocks are padded with dummy items to make them exactly $N^{1/6}$ long. The insertion of these dummy items requires us to simulate a machine with $2P$ processors and to perform a monotonic permutation that spreads out the actual data items and makes room for the dummy items. The shared key sort is then performed on this simulated machine with $2P$ processors at the expense of a factor of 2 in the running time. The third part of squaremerge, namely the sorting within buckets, consists of recursive calls. It is necessary to remove the dummy items before performing these recursive calls, as an additional factor of 2 slowdown would be incurred at each level of the recursion. The removal of the dummy items is easily accomplished with a monotonic permutation and a constant number of bitonic merges (in order to create sorted blocks of length exactly $N^{1/6}$).

10.8 Pointer-Based Communication

This section examines how pointer operations can be performed on hypercube and hypercube-derived computers. Nassimi and Sahni defined two fundamental communication primitives for implementing pointer operations that are known as the **random access write** (RAW) and the **random access read** (RAR).[166] The input to both operations is a set of N records distributed between the local memories of P processors. If $N < P$, the N lowest numbered processors will be assumed to contain one record each, while if $N \geq P$, each processor will be assumed to contain N/P records. Each record consists of a data field and a pointer field that points to another record (or is null). The records with null pointer fields will be called inactive records and the remaining records will be called active records. In a RAW, the data value from each active record i is copied to the data field of the record pointed to by record i. If more than one pointer points to the same record, the data value from the lowest numbered record is stored. In a RAR, the data value from each record i is copied to the data fields of all of the records that point to record i.

As was the case with the partial permutation problem, there are static and dynamic versions of both the RAW and RAR problems. In the static versions of the problems, the values of the pointers are known at compile time, so the compiler can figure out the most efficient solution to the problem. The time that the compiler spends in calculating this solution is not included in the analysis of the static RAW and RAR algorithms. In the dynamic versions of the problems, the pointer values are not known until the RAW or RAR must be performed, therefore, the time spent deciding how to implement the operation is included in the analysis of the algorithm. The RAW and RAR routines are very powerful communication primitives that are fundamental to the solution of many symbolic problems.

10.8.1 Dynamic RAW and RAR Operations

Nassimi and Sahni showed that the dynamic RAW and RAR operations can be solved by performing a constant number of sorts, scans, and monotonic permutations.[166] A similar algorithm was given by Ullman.[251] Nassimi and Sahni's algorithm will be reviewed here. First, consider the implementation of a dynamic RAW. Begin by creating records that consist of the original data and pointer fields of the RAW operation. These records are sorted according to their pointer fields, with null pointers being larger than any other pointers. It is assumed that the sort is a stable sort, therefore, any two records with the same pointer field will remain in the same relative order.

After the sort, each record will have to know if it is the record from the lowest numbered processor that is pointing to its given destination. A record that is from the lowest numbered processor for its given destination will be called a primary record, and the remaining active records will be called secondary records. The secondary records can be discarded because the data that they hold will not be stored by the RAW operation. The primary records can be determined during the sort by having each record note all comparisons to records with identical pointers.[166] Alternately, the primary records can be determined after the sort by performing a scan operation on the pointer values. This scan operation calculates the maximum pointer value preceding each record. Thus, a record is a primary record if and only if the value returned by the scan operation is less than the record's pointer value. Regardless of which technique is used to determine which records are primary, the primary records are then routed to their destinations by using a monotonic permutation (see Section 10.4).

Nassimi and Sahni have also shown how a similar approach can be used to accomplish a RAR operation.[166] Their RAR algorithm is basically two applications of their RAW algorithm: one to deliver requests for reading data to the data items that are being read, and the other for sending the requested data to their destinations. Specifically, copies of the records are made and these copies are sorted by their pointer fields. The location of each record at this point will be called its "sorted position." Primary records are then determined as in the RAW algorithm and these primary records are monotonically routed to where they point. Each primary record then sets its data field to the data value of the record to which it points.

Next, the primary records are monotonically routed back to their sorted positions (they have extra fields that hold their original and sorted positions). Then, a segmented scan is used to copy the data field of each primary record to the remaining records with matching pointer values (actually, in Nassimi and Sahni's RAW algorithm this segmented scan operation is merged with the previous monotonic permutation). Finally, all of the active records are returned to their original locations. This can be accomplished by sorting them according to their original locations and then performing a monotonic permutation. Alternatively, the active records can be returned to their original locations by reversing the steps in the original sort.

The key to the RAW and RAR algorithms is the initial sort of the records. The sorting of the records accomplishes two things. First, it brings together all of the records that are pointing to the same location. Once the set of records with matching pointers have been brought together, it is easy to select just one of them to perform the desired access. Second, the sort orders the records so that a monotonic permutation can be used to perform the access. The time required for sorting the records dominates the asymptotic complexity of the dynamic RAW and RAR algorithms on hypercube and hypercube-derived computers, regardless of the relationship between N and P. Therefore, a dynamic RAW or RAR of N records on a hypercube computer with P processors can be performed in $O(T\text{sort}(N, P))$ time, where $T\text{sort}(N, P)$ is the time required to sort N items on a P processor hypercube computer.

In particular, when $N^{1+1/\log\log N} \leq P$, the sparse enumeration sort (see Section 10.7.3) can be used to perform a dynamic RAW or RAR with N items in $O(\log N \log P/\log(P/N))$ time. When $N \leq P \leq N^{1+1/\log\log N}$, share-sort (see Section 10.7.4) can be used to perform a dynamic RAW or RAR with N items in $O(\log N \log\log N)$ time. Alternatively, the bitonic sort (see Section 10.7.1) can be used to obtain an $O(\log^2 N)$ time dynamic RAW or RAR algorithm with a smaller constant of proportionality. Finally, when $N > P$, sharesort (see Section 10.7.2) can be used to obtain an $O((N/P)\log N \log\log N)$ time dynamic RAW or RAR algorithm. Alternatively, a sorting algorithm based on smoothsort (see Section 10.7.2) can be used to obtain an $O((N/P)\log^2 N/\log(N/P))$ time dynamic RAW or RAR algorithm with small constants of proportionality. All of these algorithms run in the same time bounds on the hypercube-derived computers.

Finally, note that the definition of the RAW operation can be extended without changing the overall complexity of the RAW algorithm on a hypercube computer. So far, it has been said that when multiple records point to the same destination, only the data item from the highest numbered processor that points to the given destination will be stored there. Instead, it could be said that some associative binary operator "$+$" is applied to all of the data values that point to a given destination and that the plus reduction of these data values will be stored in the given destination. This form of the RAW operation can be implemented by performing the RAW algorithm described above, except that following the sort, a segmented scan operation is used to calculate the plus reduction of the data values being written to the same location.

Although the above algorithms have good performance in a worst case sense, several other algorithms have good average case performance. One such algorithm is the routing algorithm for the Connection Machine that was discussed in Section 8.5. Another such algorithm consists of using Ranade's routing algorithm (see Section 10.9) combined with Valiant and Brebner's technique of sending each item first to a random destination (see Section 10.6.2). At the present time, it is unclear which algorithms are the best in practice. More research is definitely needed in this area.

10.8.2 Static RAW and RAR Operations

The static forms of the RAW and RAR operations can be accomplished by using algorithms that are similar to the algorithms for the dynamic RAW and RAR operations. The only difference is that in the static versions of these problems, the location of each record following each sort operation is known at compile time. As a result, the static permutation algorithm given in Section 10.6.1 can be used in place of the sorting algorithm. Thus, the static RAW and RAR operations can be implemented in $O((N/P)\log N)$ time on a plain hypercube or a hypercube-derived computer.

10.8.3 Monotonic RAW and RAR Operations

A dynamic RAW or RAR operation will be said to be "monotonic" if the sequence of non-null pointers is monotonically nondecreasing. The algorithms for monotonic RAW and RAR operations are very similar to the algorithms for the unrestricted dynamic RAW and RAR operations. The only difference is that the sorts can be replaced by concentrate and distribute operations (see Section 10.4). The resulting algorithms implement the monotonic RAW and RAR operations in $O((N/P)\log N)$ time on a plain hypercube or a hypercube-derived computer.

10.8.4 Repeated RAW and RAR Operations

The above algorithms for dynamic RAW and RAR operations do not "learn" how to perform RARs and RAWs more quickly if the same request for reading or writing data is repeated. However, in some applications, multiple RAW and RAR operations have to be performed with the same set of pointers. For example, when simulating a VLSI circuit, it is common to repeatedly communicate according to the graph that describes the electrical connectivity of the circuit. In such cases, it may be preferable to use the static RAW and RAR algorithms, even though the problem is actually dynamic (the pattern of communication is not known until compile time). Assume that $N = P$. Then, it will require $O(\log^3 N \log\log N)$ time to compute the intermediate destinations for the Benes routing (see Section 10.6.1), but once these intermediate destinations have been found, successive RAWs and RARs can be performed in $O(\log N)$ time each. If more than $\log N \log\log N$ successive RAWs and RARs are needed, this approach could very well be faster overall.

10.9 Simulating PRAMs

One of the most convenient models of parallel computation is the PRAM model (see Section 3.1.1). The PRAM is a shared memory model, so it allows the algorithm designer to ignore communication issues. Because it is so convenient for algorithm designers, more parallel algorithms have been developed for the PRAM than for any other model of parallel computers. It would, therefore, be very useful to have a standard technique by which a hypercube or a hypercube-derived computer could simulate a PRAM. In this section, several techniques for performing such PRAM simulations will be reviewed.

Concentration will be on simulating the most powerful type of PRAM, namely the PRIORITY CRCW PRAM (see Section 3.1.1). In general, the number of processors in a PRAM may not equal the number of shared memory locations. As a result, two parameters will be used to describe the size of a PRAM. An "(M, N) PRAM" is a PRIORITY CRCW PRAM with M words of shared memory and N processors. (M, N) PRAMs will be considered, where $M < N$, $M = N$ and $M > N$. The case where $M < N$ is very uncommon and is included only for completeness. The case where $M = N$ is probably the most common. This is a very natural model because it allows the algorithm designer to assign a processor to each data item and to view the data items as being active. Finally, the case where $M > N$ is less common but still important. When $M > N$, the standard assumption will be made that M is polynomial in N (that is, $M \leq N^k$ for some constant k).

An (M, N) PRAM with a P processor hypercube or hypercube-derived computer will be simulated. PRAM simulation techniques can be classified according to how they map the M shared memory locations to the P processors. Three types of memory organizations, namely direct mapped, replicated, and hashed, will be considered.

10.9.1 Direct Mapped Memory

Certainly, the simplest memory organization is a direct mapped one. In this scheme, each of the M shared memory locations is stored in one location, and successive shared memory locations are stored in adjacent locations. Specifically, when $M \leq P$, the M shared memory locations of the PRAM are assigned, one per processor, to the M first processors in the hypercube. When $M > P$, the M shared memory locations are stored M/P per processor, with shared memory location i being stored in (local) memory location $i \bmod P$ of processor floor(i/P). The RAW and RAR algorithms given in Section 10.8.1 can then be used to simulate the PRAM's accesses to shared memory.

First, consider the case where $M \leq P$. In this case, the PRAM's read accesses can be simulated by performing a RAR with N records on a P processor hypercube. Similarly, the PRAM's write accesses can be simulated by performing a RAW with N records on a P processor hypercube. Finally, during one step of a PRAM program, each processor can perform a constant number of calculations on its local data. These local operations can be simulated in $O(N/P)$ time on a hypercube. Thus if $M \leq P$, each step of an (M, N) PRAM step can be simulated on a P processor hypercube or hypercube-derived computer in $O((N/P) \log N \log\log N)$ time when $P \leq N$, in $O(\log N \log\log N)$ time when $N \leq P \leq N^{1+1/\log\log N}$, and in $O(\log N \log P / \log(P/N))$ time when $N^{1+1/\log\log N} \leq P$.

Now, consider the case where $M > P$. If $N \geq M$ (as is common), each shared memory access can be implemented by performing a RAR and a RAW with N records on a P processor hypercube. Therefore, each (M, N) PRAM step can be simulated in $O((N/P) \log N \log\log N)$ time by using sharesort to perform the sorts of N records. A more practical alternative is to use the smoothsort-based sorting algorithm, in which case an $O((N/P) \log^2 N / \log(N/P))$ time simulation is obtained. The constants of proportionality are quite small with this approach, so it deserves real consideration in practice. This case is also probably the most important one in practice, as it is very common for N and M to be equal and to be larger than P.

Finally, if $M > P$ and $M > N$, there are possible problems with congestion. For example, consider the case where $M = P^2$ and $N = P$. In this case, P shared memory locations are assigned to each hypercube processor. However, a single PRAM step could require that all P shared memory locations assigned to hypercube processor number 0 be read. Because a hypercube processor can only access one of its memory locations at a time, such a PRAM step would require time proportional to P. As a result, the direct mapped memory is probably not the best scheme to use in such a situation.

10.9.2 Replicated Memory

Upfal and Wigderson[254] developed a PRAM simulation technique for the case $M > P$ and $P = N$. Their algorithm avoids congestion by making $O(\log M)$ copies of each shared memory location and storing them in different processors. The rule that determines the locations of the $O(M \log M)$ copies of shared memory locations is nonconstructive and is based on the existence of certain graphs. The idea is to use the multiple copies so that if some of the copies of a shared memory location cannot be accessed due to congestion, the remaining copies will be accessed and the PRAM simulation can continue.

Specifically, when a shared memory location has to be written, a majority of the $O(\log M)$ copies of that memory location have to be updated to the new value. Also, each copy of the memory location has a time-stamp that tells when the copy was last updated. When a shared memory location has to be read, a majority of the $O(\log M)$ copies of that memory location have to be accessed. The time-stamps of the accessed copies are compared and the value stored in the copy with the most recent time stamp is used as the value of the read operation. Because both read and write operations access a majority of the copies, each read operation is guaranteed to return the correct (most recent) value. Upfal and Wigderson showed that this technique can be used to implement a single step of an (M, N) PRAM on a bounded degree computer with $P = N$ processors in $O(\log^2 N \log\log N)$ time.[254] The bounded degree computer that they use is based on the AKS sorting network,[5] and is not a hypercube-derived topology. However, by using the sorting and routing algorithms described earlier in this chapter, their technique can be used to implement a single step of an (M, N) PRAM on a hypercube or hypercube-derived computer with $P = N$ processors in $O(\log^2 N \log\log^2 N)$ time.

10.9.3 Hashed Memory

A second technique for avoiding congestion when $M > P$ and $P = N$ was developed by Melhorn and Vishkin. Their technique uses only one copy of each shared memory location. The shared memory locations are assigned to the processors randomly, according to a universal hashing function.[40] Because the memory locations are assigned to the processors by hashing, it is extremely unlikely that any given PRAM step will require too many accesses to a single processor.

Karlin and Upfal combined the idea of hashing the shared memory with randomized routing techniques to obtain a probabilistic simulation of a PRAM on a BF (butterfly) computer.[125] Their simulation implements any T steps of an (M, N) PRAM program on an N processor BF computer in $O(T \log M)$ time with high probability. Karlin and Upfal's algorithm is easiest to explain when the PRAM being simulated is an EREW PRAM. In this case, Upfal's randomized $O(\log N)$ time routing algorithm (see Section 10.6.2) is used to send each read or write request to the processor holding the desired shared memory location. Note that it is possible for several requests to be directed to the same processor (because it holds multiple shared memory locations that are being accessed), but Karlin and Upfal were able to show that Upfal's routing algorithm still terminates in $O(\log N)$ time with high probability. Occasionally, it is possible that a PRAM step cannot be simulated in $O(\log N)$ time because too many shared memory locations must be accessed from a single processor. In such situations, the entire shared memory must be rehashed (that is, assigned to processors according to a new randomly selected hash function). The rehashing of the memory is very expensive [requiring time proportional to $(M/N)\log N$], but it is infrequent enough that it does not affect the overall time bounds for the PRAM simulation.

The above algorithm performs an EREW PRAM simulation on a BF computer. In order to simulate a PRIORITY CRCW PRAM, Karlin and Upfal first sort the read and write requests according to their destinations. Then, the requests that have a common destination are combined into a single request as was done in the RAW and RAR algorithms given in Section 10.8.1. Finally, these requests are routed with Upfal's routing algorithm as described above.

Another (M, N) PRAM simulation algorithm based on hashing the shared memory was created by Ranade.[201] This algorithm also implements any T steps of an (M, N) PRAM program on an N processor BF computer in $O(T\log M)$ time with high probability. However, Ranade's algorithm is a significant improvement because it does not require costly priority queues in each processor, and the queues are of constant size. Also, it has the advantage of being able to implement PRIORITY CRCW PRAM algorithms directly, without first sorting the requests to eliminate hot spots.

First, consider how the write requests are handled in Ranade's algorithm. Recall that the processors in a BF computer are arranged in rows and columns. The route of any data item consists of three phases. In phase 1, it travels within its row to successively higher numbered columns until it crosses the wraparound connections to column 0. In phase 2, it uses ascend routing to go to the destination row. Finally, in phase 3, it travels within the row to the destination column. Each processor in the physical BF network performs routing for all three phases. However, items that are in different phases do not interact with one another, so it will be convenient to view each physical processor as being three logical processors, one devoted to each phase. The algorithm will be described in terms of these logical processors.

The key to Ranade's algorithm is the scheduling of the data items. Each logical processor only transmits an item when it is sure that no other item with the same destination will pass through it. Thus, whenever two items have paths that pass through the same logical processor, they will be combined at that processor. The process of combining messages is trivial when performing a write (it just requires ignoring all but one of the items), but it will be shown that it is more involved when implementing a read.

In order to let the logical processors know when they can safely send an item, the sequence of items leaving each logical processor is sorted in ascending order according to destination. For example, consider a logical processor performing phase 2 routing. It has two input ports, each of which has an associated queue. At each step, it examines the two items at the head of each queue and sends out the item with the smaller destination. As a result, the items that it transmits are guaranteed to be monotonically increasing in terms of destinations. The logical processors for phase 1 and phase 3 use an identical algorithm, except for the definition of the input ports. Specifically, in phase 1, one of the input ports corresponds to items that are just beginning to be routed and the other input port receives items from the adjacent phase 1 logical processor in the same row. In phase 3, one of the input ports corresponds to items that have just completed their phase 2 routing and the other input port receives items from the adjacent phase 3 logical processor in the same row.

Note that the phase 1 and phase 3 logical processors have only one output, but that the phase 2 logical processors have two outputs. When a phase 2 logical processor sends an item out of one of its outputs, it also sends a "ghost item" with the same destination value through its other output. This ghost item carries no data and does not have to be delivered. It is only used to tell the logical processor that receives it that all subsequent items will be to destinations larger than the ghost's destination. Thus, ghosts can help to prevent unnecessary waiting. When a logical processor receives a ghost, it transmits the ghost over both of its outputs if the ghost destination is smaller than the destination at the head of the other queue. Otherwise, a logical processor that receives a ghost can discard the ghost without retransmitting it. Ranade has shown that this system of keeping the items sorted according to destination, plus using ghost items, gives a routing scheme that terminates in $O(\log N)$ time with overwhelming probability.

The algorithm for handling read requests has two halves. In the first half, the read requests are routed to their destinations as in the write algorithm described above. Whenever two read requests with the same destination are present in the same logical processor, they are combined to form a single read request. Thus, the read requests to a single destination form a binary tree. In the second half, the requested data are routed back to the requesting processors by reversing the operations of the first half. Wherever two read requests were combined in the first half, two copies of the requested data are created in the second half in order to satisfy both requests. Thus, the requests are broadcast back over the tree created in the first half. In order to perform this broadcast correctly, each logical processor has to maintain a queue of bits that defines the tree's structure. This queue will contain $O(\log N)$ entries, but only $O(\log N)$ bits, so its memory requirements are no greater than a constant number of $O(\log N)$ bit data items.

Ranade's algorithm has fairly small constants of proportionality in its running time, and its hardware requirements are not great. Therefore, it seems to be a promising algorithm for practical use. However, the hashing of the memory could cause occasional hot spots that would require rehashing the entire memory. Also, the hashing of the memory destroys any locality or regularity in the algorithm, both of which can sometimes be exploited to reduce communication costs. More research is needed to determine which routing algorithm is the best in practice.

10.10 Data-Dependent Parallel Prefix

In Section 10.3, the data-independent parallel prefix problem was examined. Now, a related but more difficult problem will be considered, namely, the data-dependent parallel prefix problem. The input to the data-dependent parallel prefix problem is an array A containing N data values, an associated array B containing N pointers to data values (which may be null), and an associative binary operator $+$ with identity 0. The pointers form a set of linear linked lists. The problem is to calculate, for each of the lists, the plus reduction of each of the prefixes of the list. That is, if $X = x_1, x_2, \ldots,$ x_k is a sequence of integers such that for all $i > 1$, $B(x_i) = x_{i-1}$ and $B(x_1)$ is null, then for each i where $l \leq i \leq k$, the problem is to calculate $A(x_1) + A(x_2) + \cdots + A(x_{i-1})$.

The data-dependent parallel prefix problem is used as a subroutine in many other problems. For example, there is a well-known technique, called the Euler tour technique, that transforms a tree into a linked list.[245] The data-dependent parallel prefix operation can then be applied to this linked list in order to calculate functions of the tree such as the preorder and postorder numberings of the vertices in the tree and the number of descendents of each vertex in the tree.[128]

Another problem that is closely related to the data-dependent parallel prefix problem is the list reduction problem. The input to the list reduction problem is identical to the input to the data-dependent parallel prefix problem, except that the pointer fields may form either linear lists or circular lists. The problem is to calculate, for each record, the maximum of the data fields in the list containing that record.

The list reduction problem can be solved simply in $O(\log N)$ time on an EREW PRAM of with N processors.[87] Fortune and Wyllie's algorithm consists of $\log N$ stages. In each stage, every item examines the data field in its predecessor (the item to which it points). If that predecessor's data field is larger than its own, its data field is set to equal its predecessor's data field. Then, each item sets its pointer to equal its predecessor's pointer. The updating of the pointers causes each pointer to "jump-over" the item to which it formerly pointed, so this operation is often called "pointer-jumping." If an item has no predecessor (its pointer is null), it becomes inactive for the remainder of the algorithm. It is easy to prove that after i stages, each item contains the largest data field from a set of 2^i adjacent items.

By using the $O(\log N \log\log N)$ time nonconstructive RAR and RAW algorithms discussed in Section 10.8.1 to simulate the above EREW PRAM algorithm, an $O(\log^2 N \log\log N)$ time algorithm for a hypercube or hypercube-derived computer with $P = N$ processors is obtained. However, Cypher has created a constructive algorithm for the data-dependent parallel prefix problem with the same time bounds.[51] This algorithm also has the advantage of being very efficient when $N > P$. Specifically, it requires $O(\log^2 N \log\log N)$ time when $P \leq N \leq \log\log P \log\log\log P$ and $O((N/P)\log^2 N/\log(N/P))$ time when $N \geq \log\log P \log\log\log P$.

Cypher's algorithm is based on an optimal PRAM algorithm for the data-dependent parallel prefix problem developed by Cole and Vishkin.[46] In the first half of Cole and Vishkin's algorithm, the items in each list are removed from the list until the list is empty. When an item is removed from a list the item that points to it is made to jump over it and point to the next item in the list. After an item is removed from a list, it remains inactive until it is replaced during the second half of the algorithm. The first half of the algorithm consists of $O(\log N)$ stages, each of which removes at least one-fourth of the items from each list. The second half of the algorithm replaces the items that were removed during the first half. The second half is essentially the reverse of the first half, with the items that were removed during stage i of the first half being replaced during the i-th to last stage in the second half.

When an item is removed from a list, it passes its value to the item that precedes it in the list. Thus, the item that is removed and the item that precedes it can be viewed as being children of a single node that contains the information from both of these items. As a result, the first half of the algorithm creates a binary tree similar to the tree created in the scan algorithm presented in Section 10.3.1, except that it might not be a complete binary tree. Once again, during the first half of the algorithm, each node in the tree stores the value passed up to it from its left child. During the second half of the algorithm, the items are replaced in the lists in the opposite order in which they were removed. As each item is replaced in the list, it exchanges data with the item that precedes it in the list. Specifically, it performs the same calculations as were performed during the second half of the scan algorithm. Therefore, at the end of the second half, all of the desired reductions will have been calculated.

A key operation in Cole and Vishkin's algorithm is the selection of the items to be removed from the lists during the first half. At each stage, at least one-fourth of the items in each list are marked for removal. However, no two items that are adjacent in a list can be marked for removal. This is because the operation of making the pointer from the following item jump over, the removed item will fail if two adjacent items are removed. Cole and Vishkin use an interesting "symmetry breaking" operation to select which items should be removed. This symmetry breaking operation involves calculations on the binary representations of the pointers.

Because Cole and Vishkin's algorithm reduces the number of active records as it progresses, it lends itself to an efficient hypercube implementation. In particular, when $N < P$ items remain $O(\log N \log P/\log(P/N))$ time dynamic RAW and RAR algorithms (see Section 10.8.1) can be used to simulate each PRAM step. Cypher's hypercube algorithm is based on this type of simulation, plus a few modifications that improve the performance of the symmetry breaking operation on the hypercube.[51] These modifications to the symmetry breaking operation were first used by Ja'Ja' and Ryu.[116]

10.11 Communication Primitives For Other Types of Hypercubes

So far, the focus has been on communication primitives for plain hypercube computers. These communication primitives have the advantage that they can also be implemented on the bounded degree hypercube-derived computers in the same time bounds. However, many of the commercial hypercube computers are asynchronous and many have some form of strong communication (the ability to send multiple messages from a single processor simultaneously). How to perform communication on these other types of hypercubes will be considered briefly.

First, consider a synchronous hypercube with strong communication. When there are at least $\log P$ data items per processor, it is often possible to obtain a factor of $\log P$ speed-up over the algorithm for a plain hypercube. For example, consider an ascend algorithm where $N = P \log P$. An array location i can be assigned to memory location $i \bmod P$ of processor floor(i/P). The processing for the loglog P least significant bits is all local and requires no communication. Then, the processing for the remaining bit positions is done in a pipelined manner. First, the least significant dimension of the hypercube is used for the array locations stored in memory location 0 of the respective processors. Next, the second dimension of the hypercube is used for these same array locations while the least significant dimension is used for the array locations stored in memory location 1. This procedure is continued, with the array locations stored in memory position i using the least significant dimension of the hypercube at stage i. The entire ascend algorithm for $N = P \log P$, thus, requires only $O(\log P)$ time for communication.

Now, consider an asynchronous hypercube computer. One way to program such a machine is to use the synchronous hypercube algorithms given above. If the processors all run at approximately the same speed, then the asynchronous machine will perform just like a synchronous one. A barrier synchronization can be used to resynchronize the processors when they begin to drift apart. Even if the processors do not operate at approximately the same speed, the algorithms for synchronous computers could be used to assure an even load on all of the communication links. For example, the Benes routing algorithm (see Section 10.6.1) guarantees that, at most, two items cross each communication link in each direction.

Another way to program an asynchronous machine is to use communication paths that do not overlap. Then regardless of the relative speeds of the processors, no collisions will occur. For example, algorithms for broadcasting data from one processor to all the remaining processors that use edge-disjoint spanning trees have been created by Johnsson and Ho.[120]

CHAPTER 11

Algorithms for Hypercube Computers

This chapter will study how several problems in image processing and scientific computing can be solved on hypercube computers. All of the problems will be solved using a plain hypercube computer (see Chapter 10) and the hypercube-derived computers (see Chapter 9). Unless stated otherwise, it will be assumed that $N = P$ and that each processor has a constant number of words of memory, each consisting of $O(\log N)$ bits. Many of the algorithms in this chapter will make extensive use of the communication primitives given in the previous chapter.

11.1 Table Lookup Operation

This is the same problem as was discussed in Section 5.1. If the table has not been loaded in the processors, the simple $O(V)$ time algorithm presented for mesh connected computers is the best possible for a plain hypercube computer. If each processor has $O(V)$ memory and independent addressing, and if the table has been loaded in advance, it is of course possible to solve the problem in constant time.

Finally, if each processor has a constant amount of memory and the table can be preloaded, an algorithm similar to the one presented in Section 5.8 can be used. Specifically, let V' be the smallest power of 2 greater than or equal to V. Divide the processors into P/V' groups (it will be assumed that $V \le P$), each of which consists of V' consecutively numbered processors. Store the i-th entry of the lookup table in the i-th processor in each group. Then the RAR algorithms given in Section 10.8 can be used to perform the table lookup operation in $O(\log V \log\log V)$ time. Alternatively, the more practical bitonic sort-based RAR algorithm could be used to give an $O(\log^2 V)$ time algorithm.

11.2 $M \times M$ Convolution

An $O(M^2)$ time plain mesh connected computer algorithm for performing an $M \times M$ convolution was presented in Section 5.2. Therefore, a hypercube with independent communication, or a hypercube-derived computer, can use the mesh connected computer simulation techniques given in Section 10.2 to perform an $M \times M$ convolution in $O(M^2)$ time. Because a plain hypercube can implement a single operation of a plain mesh connected computer in $O(\log N)$ time, the same algorithm can also be used to calculate an $M \times M$ convolution in $O(M^2 \log N)$ time on a plain hypercube computer.

However, an $O(M^2 \log^* M + \log N)$ time convolution algorithm for a plain hypercube was created by Prasanna Kumar.[192] The algorithm first divides the image into $M \times M$ squares (it is assumed that M is a power of 2). Then, all of the data required to calculate the convolution for the pixels in a given square are moved to that square in $O(\log N)$ time. Next, the data items in each $M \times M$ square are circulated so that each item visits all of the PEs in the square. This circulation is performed by a complex recursive procedure that requires $O(M^2 \log^* M)$ time. It is not clear if this algorithm is faster than the $O(M^2 \log N)$ time algorithm given above for typical values of M and N.

Finally, an $M \times M$ convolution can be calculated in $O(M^2 + \log N)$ time on a hypercube with $O(M)$ words of memory per PE and independent addressing. Algorithms with this performance appear in.[78,79,192] All of these algorithms assume that the image has been stored in the PEs according to a row-major ordering. They achieve their efficiency by shifting the image in a pattern determined by a Gray code. Although this shifting pattern is very efficient, it has the disadvantage that, at a given time, different PEs are accessing different neighbors. For instance, one PE could contain a pixel from the next higher row, while at the same time, a different PE could contain a pixel from two rows below. As a result, following a shift operation, it is impossible for the controller to broadcast a single weight that can be multiplied by the pixels currently in the PEs. Instead, the $O(M)$ words of memory are used to store $O(M)$ shifted versions of the image, and the independent addressing is used to retrieve the correct pixel in each PE.

11.3 Finding the Value and Location of a Global Maximum

The location and value of a global maximum can be found in $O(\log N)$ time on a plain hypercube computer. One simple way to do this is to use a scan operation (see Section 10.3.1). Each processor creates a record consisting of its data value and its processor number. The binary operator $+$ is defined so that it returns the record with the larger data value (or either record in the case of matching data values). This gives the highest numbered processor the value and location of a maximum. This result can then be sent to the other processors in $O(\log N)$ time by using the broadcast operation (see Section 10.3.3) in the reverse direction (from the highest to the lowest numbered processor).

11.4 Histogram

Several algorithms have been designed for calculating a histogram with V values on a hypercube with P PEs. First, consider the case where $V \leq P$. A simple algorithm is based on the use of the "recursive doubling" technique presented in Ref. 227. This algorithm requires $O(V + \log N)$ time. Although it uses only uniform addressing and communication, it does require that each PE have $O(V)$ words of memory. Each PE has an array of V elements that is initialized to all zeroes. The algorithm first places a 1 in the location of the array corresponding to the value of the pixel it contains. This step takes V store operations because independent addressing is not allowed. Then PEs that differ in the most significant bit of their indices communicate with each other. The PE with the higher index receives the $V/2$ highest elements from the other PE's array, and the PE with the lower index receives the $V/2$ lowest elements from the other PE's array. The PEs then add the received values to their stored values. Now each PE has an array of $V/2$ elements that is the result of this addition. Next, PEs that differ in the next most significant bit communicate and trade half of their $V/2$ element arrays. After this stage, each PE has a $V/4$ element array. This process is repeated $\log V$ times, at which point each PE has an array with only one element. If $V = P$, this is the desired histogram. If $V < P$, the single values are combined using $\log P - \log V$ additional shifts and adds.

An asymptotically faster algorithm for a more restrictive model of hypercube is given by Cohn and Haddad.[43] Their algorithm takes $O(\log^2 V + \log N)$ time on a plain hypercube computer. The algorithm can be divided into two halves. In the first half, the data items are divided into groups of K^3 consecutive items and the key reduction of each of these groups is calculated in parallel. In the second half, the results from the first half are merged together to obtain the final answer.

The first half consists of three steps. First, each group of K^3 consecutive records is sorted according to the key values. This is accomplished in $O(\log^2 K)$ time by using a bitonic sort (see Section 10.7.1). Second, a segmented scan operation (see Section 10.3.2) is used to calculate the number of records within each group that have the same key value. This operation requires $O(\log K)$ time. Third, in each group, the $J \leq K$ values in that group that were calculated during the second step are moved to the J lowest numbered processors in the group. This is accomplished in $O(\log K)$ time by using a Rank operation (see Section 10.3.3) and concentrate operation (see Section 10.4).

The second half consists of $(\log N)/(\log K)$ stages. Each stage merges together K lists of K or fewer values each. The merging is done by using a three-step process that is similar to the three-step process used in the first half of the algorithm. The only difference is that because so few processors contain active data, the sorting operation can be performed more efficiently. In particular, K^4 processors are devoted to merging K lists of K or fewer values each, so the sparse enumeration sort (see Section 10.7.3) can be used to perform the sort in $O(\log K)$ time. Thus, each stage requires $O(\log K)$ time and the second half of the algorithm requires $O(\log N)$ time. The entire algorithm, therefore, runs in $O(\log^2 K + \log N)$ time. The constant of proportionality in the running time of this algorithm is moderate, so it is unclear if it is faster than the simple recursive doubling algorithm in practice.

Of course Sharesort (see Section 10.7.4) could be used instead of the bitonic sort. The resulting algorithm is less practical, but has an $O(\log K \log\log K + \log N)$ running time. In addition to these algorithms, a histogram algorithm for the Connection Machine can be found in Ref. 156.

11.5 Hough (or Radon) Transform

In Section 5.5, the Hough and Radon transforms were defined as consisting of Q projections of an $N^{1/2} \times N^{1/2}$ image. An $O(N^{1/2} + Q)$ time algorithm for calculating these projections on a mesh connected computer was given. Therefore, an $O(N^{1/2} + Q)$ time algorithm for a hypercube with independent communication and for a hypercube-derived computer can be obtained by using the mesh connected computer simulation techniques given is Section 10.2. Also, because each operation of a mesh connected computer can be implemented on a plain hypercube in $O(\log N)$ time, this approach yields an $O(N^{1/2} \log N + Q \log N)$ time algorithm.

Another approach, which is used in Ref. 156, is to use RAW operations (see Section 10.8). First, it will be shown how each projection can be calculated separately. For each projection, every PE first calculates which band it lies in. Then, a RAW is performed, where the band number is used as the pointer field and the gray level is used as the data field. When multiple PEs point to the same location, all of the gray levels from those PEs are added together. Because each RAW operation requires $O(\log N \log\log N)$ time, this approach yields an $O(Q \log N \log\log N)$ time algorithm. A more practical $O(Q \log^2 N)$ time algorithm is obtained if the bitonic sort is used within the RAW operations. An advantage of using RAW operations is that the same algorithm works equally well for generalized versions of the Hough transform, where circular or elliptical bands are used instead of straight bands.

11.6 Dense Matrix Multiplication

An algorithm for multiplying a pair of $N^{1/2} \times N^{1/2}$ matrices on an N processor mesh connected computer in $O(N^{1/2})$ time was shown in Section 5.6. Of course, a hypercube with weak independent communication or a hypercube-derived computer could simulate a mesh connected computer to obtain the same performance. In fact, Dekel, Nassimi, and Sahni have shown that even a plain hypercube can perform matrix multiplication in $O(N^{1/2})$ time.[69] Furthermore, their algorithm is quite simple and practical.

Let $\mathbf{A}$ and $\mathbf{B}$ be the matrices to be multiplied, and let $\mathbf{C}$ be the resultant matrix. Each entry $c_{i,j}$ in $\mathbf{C}$ is the sum, over all values of k from 1 through $N^{1/2}$, of $a_{i,k} * b_{k,j}$. In other words, in order to calculate $c_{i,j}$ the entries in row i of $\mathbf{A}$ must be multiplied by the corresponding entries in column j of $\mathbf{B}$.

Recall that the mesh algorithm has two phases. In the first phase, each row i of $\mathbf{A}$ is shifted (cyclically) to the left i times and each column j of $\mathbf{B}$ is shifted (cyclically) upwards j times. This aligns matrices $\mathbf{A}$ and $\mathbf{B}$ so that corresponding entries are stored in the same PE. Specifically, at the end of the first phase each entry, $a_{i,j}$ is stored in PE (i, k) where $k = i + j \bmod N^{1/2}$, and each entry $b_{i,j}$ is stored in PE (k, j) where $k = i + j \bmod N^{1/2}$. Then the second phase calculates each entry $c_{i,j}$ in $\mathbf{C}$ by successively shifting $\mathbf{A}$ to the left and $\mathbf{B}$ upwards so that all pairs of the form $a_{i,k}$ and $b_{k,j}$ visit PE (i, j).

The plain hypercube algorithm is almost identical. The only difference is in the pattern of the shifts within the rows of $\mathbf{A}$ and the columns of $\mathbf{B}$. The plain hypercube algorithm starts with the matrices $\mathbf{A}$ and $\mathbf{B}$ stored in row major order. The PE that initially holds $a_{i,j}$ and $b_{i,j}$ will be referred to as PE (i, j) (thus, it is actually PE number $iN^{1/2} + j$ in the standard hypercube numbering). The first phase of the hypercube algorithm sends each entry $a_{i,j}$ to PE (i, k), where $k = i$ XOR j and each entry $b_{i,j}$ to PE (k, j) where $k = i$ XOR j (where XOR is the bitwise exclusive or operator). This communication is implemented with ascend routing (see Section 10.4). It is straightforward to show that no collisions can occur during this ascend routing.

Then, the second phase of the hypercube algorithm shifts the rows of $\mathbf{A}$ and the columns of $\mathbf{B}$ according to a Gray code pattern.[78] Specifically, after h steps of the second phase, each entry $a_{i,j}$ is stored in PE (i, k) where $k = i$ XOR j XOR Gray(h) and each entry $b_{i,j}$ is stored in PE (k, j) where $k = i$ XOR j XOR Gray(h), where Gray(h) is the h-th element of a Gray code sequence. After each shift of $\mathbf{A}$ and $\mathbf{B}$, the new pair of entries in each PE are multiplied and added to a running total variable, as was the case in the mesh algorithm.

It is clear that the above pattern of shifts brings all pairs of the form $a_{i,k}$ and $b_{k,j}$ to PE (i,j). Also, because successive elements of a Gray code sequence differ in only one bit position, each shift uses only direct hypercube connections and the entire set of $N^{1/2}$ shifts requires only $O(N^{1/2})$ time on a plain hypercube. It is less clear that the entire set of $N^{1/2}$ shifts can also be implemented in $O(N^{1/2})$ time, but this turns out to be the case when the standard binary reflected Gray code is used.

11.7 Image Connected Component Labeling

The connected components of a binary image can be labeled in $O(\log^2 N)$ time on a plain hypercube computer.[59] The algorithm uses a divide-and-conquer approach similar to Nassimi and Sahni's symbolic labeling algorithm discussed in Section 5.9.[169] The N pixel image is divided into $N^{1/2}$ square windows each containing $N^{1/2}$ pixels. These $N^{1/2}$ pixel windows are labeled recursively. At this point, the connected components are correctly labeled except for possible inconsistencies along the borders between windows. These inconsistencies are then removed by using a graph theoretic connected component labeling algorithm.[226]

That graph theoretic algorithm requires $O(\log N)$ RAW and RAR operations. Because there are only $O(N^{3/4})$ pixels that lie on the borders of the windows, and because only these border pixels send or receive data during the RAW and RAR operations, each RAW and RAR operation can be completed in $O(\log N)$ time by using the routines presented in Section 10.8.1. As a result, the entire algorithm requires just $O(\log^2 N)$ time. However, the constant of proportionality in the running time is large, so the simple $O(N^{1/2})$ time algorithms for mesh connected computers (see Section 5.9) are probably nearly as fast for realistic image sizes.

11.8 Sparse Vector-Matrix Multiplication

This section will show how a (possibly sparse) row vector can be multiplied by a sparse matrix on a plain hypercube computer. Of course, this algorithm could be applied repeatedly to multiply two sparse matrices. Let $\mathbf{A} = (a_j)$, $0 \le j < M$, be a row vector and let $\mathbf{B} = (b_{i,j})$, $0 \le i,\ j < M$ be a sparse matrix. The goal is to calculate the row vector $\mathbf{C} = \mathbf{A} * \mathbf{B}$. It will be assumed that there are at most P nonzero elements in $\mathbf{B}$ and that $M \le P$. The nonzero values of $\mathbf{A}$ are held in records with two fields $\langle j, a_j \rangle$ where j indicates the column number. The nonzero values of $\mathbf{B}$ are held in records with three fields $\langle i, j, b_{i,j} \rangle$ where i and j indicate the row and column number.

Note that the sparse matrix $\mathbf{B}$ can be put into row major order by sorting the records in $\mathbf{B}$ with the primary key being the row number and the secondary key being the column number. Similarly, $\mathbf{B}$ can be put into column major order by sorting with the column number as the primary key and the row number as the secondary key.

An algorithm to calculate $C = A * B$ is given below.

- Sort the **A** records so that they are stored one per processor.
- Send each **A** record of the form $\langle j, a_j \rangle$ to PE j. This can be accomplished with a monotonic permutation (see Section 10.4).
- Put **B** into row major order by performing a sort as described above.
- Have each **B** record of the form $\langle i, j, b_{i,j} \rangle$ read a_i from PE i. This can be accomplished with a monotonic RAR (see Section 10.8.3).
- Each PE with a **B** record multiplies a_i by $b_{i,j}$. Attach the result to the **B** record. This is a local computation.
- Put **B** into column major order by performing a sort as described above.
- Add together the products of the form $a_i * b_{i,j}$ within columns of **B**. This is a segmented scan operation (see Section 10.3.2).
- Send each sum from column i in the previous step to PE i. This is a monotonic permutation (see Section 10.4). This completes the calculation of **C**.

The complexity of this algorithm is the same as the complexity of sorting, so it can be accomplished in $O(\log N \log\log N)$ time on a plain hypercube computer [or in $O(\log^2 N)$ time if the more practical bitonic sort is used]. If the bitonic sort is used, the algorithm is very practical as all of the subroutines have small constants in their running times. Also, notice that only one multiplication step is needed.

11.9 Particle Simulations

This section will describe algorithms for simulating systems of particles. These algorithms provide examples of how the communication primitives in Chapter 10 can be used to solve complex applications. The computational issues will be abstracted from the application, therefore, it is not necessary to be familiar with the physics involved.

This simulation follows various physical laws describing the behavior of a system of M molecules. The applicability of these computer simulations is widely known in physics and chemistry.[14,261] Although the algorithms of this section can be extended to work on a Brownian dynamics model, the presentation will deal with classical molecular dynamics simulations only.

Consider a two-dimensional box with M molecules. It is assumed that there will be at most K molecules in each smaller $C \times C$ box where C is the maximum distance allowed for molecular interaction. This cut-off distance is used due to the negligible effect that interatomic interactions have on the potential of the system for pairs of molecules further than $2C$ apart. Each particle has velocity v_i, mass m, and position (x_i, y_i, z_i) at a certain time. Although the general problem is truly three-dimensional, a two-dimensional example is considered here for simplicity, but with no loss of generality.

Following a molecular dynamics formulation, the M particles obey classical mechanics defined by a Hamiltonian H,

$$H = \frac{1}{2} \sum_{i=1}^{M} m_i v_i^2 + \sum_{i>j} V_{ij}, \tag{2}$$

where the first term corresponds to the kinetic energy and the second one to the potential energy. The simulation consists of applying the classical dynamical equations and updating the parameters of the particles. A feature of this is that the temperature of the system is kept constant by normalizing the velocities at each step. The interaction potential is computed by using the Lennard-Jones potential function. In those terms, the instantaneous forces at each point are the gradient of the potential.

From a computational standpoint, the following issues are relevant:

- The instantaneous temperature should be kept constant. To this end, velocities are normalized at each iteration so that the kinetic energy remains constant. This involves a global computation since the total kinetic energy of the system has to be computed.
- All pairs of molecules at distance less than C must be taken into consideration for determining the next state of the system (according to Lennard-Jones 12:6 potential function).
- Update of instantaneous parameters involves simple computations for all interacting molecules (the force F_i, the aceleration, and the velocity, for each molecule i).

The main algorithm is divided into two phases: the *setup phase* and the *running phase*. The setup phase describes the initial conditions of molecules and processors. The main characteristics are as follows. Only one molecule will be assigned per processor. Each processor will hold a record containing relevant data $(x_i, y_i, m, v_i, F_i, \ldots)$. At the beginning of the setup phase, molecule coordinates are chosen at random (it is assumed that there is a known bound K on the maximum number of molecules per $C \times C$ box). The setup phase consists of assigning the molecules of the $C \times C$ boxes into groups of consecutive PEs for further processing in the running phase.

Place the molecules of each box in Groups of K consecutive PEs:

- This is accomplished by sorting with respect to the x_i coordinate of the molecule position.
- Partition the PEs in "bands" of width C.
- Sort each band independently by using the y_i coordinate of the molecule positions.
- A few monotonic RAWs and RARs and a static permutation complete this step.

The fact that the molecules corresponding to each physical $C \times C$ box are in consecutive PEs greatly improves the running phase of the algorithm. This is because only neighboring boxes to each $C \times C$ box have to be used in the update of the molecule parameters.

Three basic steps are involved in the running phase:

- *Communication:* Every group of PEs holding a box of molecules gets one neighboring box. This is accomplished by a permutation. There are eight different permutations corresponding to the North, East, West, Northeast, Northwest, Southeast, Southwest, and South neighbor boxes. Recall that the physically neighboring boxes are not placed in consecutive PEs of the computer. This communication step can be done in $O(\log P)$ time since K is known in advance, and hence, the structure of the communication is described by a static permutation.

- *Update Molecule Parameters:* Each group holding the two boxes of molecules computes the interatomic interactions and updates parameters for the molecules of the current box. The complexity of this step is $O(K)$ communications and $O(K)$ computations. If there are enough "free" processors, this can be brought down to $O(\log K)$ communications and computing (for example, $K = 32$, $M = 10,000$, $P = 1,000,000$).

- *Update Kinetic Energy:* The instantaneous temperature should be kept constant, and hence, the velocities of the particles are normalized by a factor. This factor is computed from the kinetic energy of the system shown in Eq. (2). This computation requires simple global communication and can be accomplished in $O(\log P)$ time.

Note that no dynamic unrestricted RAWs or RARs are necessary. This feature was fully exploited in a computer specially designed for such applications, called the Spark machine, where a Benes network implements the above permutations.[14]

A final remark is in order. After a number of iterations, some molecules will change boxes, therefore, the sorting steps of the setup phase must be repeated to account for these migrations. This sorting is, in fact, the bottleneck of the algorithm. However, it is expected that the number of migrations would not be critical, and therefore, the sorting operation will be used only occasionally.

11.10 Quantum Chromodynamics

Another physics problem that has received great attention is the simulation of quantum-chromodynamics systems.[19] In this problem, the main computation is an integral involving an enormous number of variables. These integrals arise often in physics simulations. A possible technique for integration of functions with a large number of variables is based on Monte Carlo techniques.[98]

Parallel Monte Carlo methods can exploit a large number of processors at different computational stages such as in the evaluation of the primary or the secondary estimators.[23] A typical example in physics involve the evaluation of an integral of the form:

$$\int f(x_1,\ldots,x_N)\,dp(x_1,\ldots,x_N), \tag{4}$$

where $p(x_1,\ldots,x_N)$ is a probability measure. A standard approach consists of the following steps

- Generate $X^i = (x_1^i,\ldots,x_N^i)$ randomly according to probability measure p.
- Compute primary estimate $f(X^i)$.
- Compute secondary estimate: $(1/M)\sum_{i=1}^{M} f(X^i)$.

As was stated above, parallelism can be exploited at different stages of the algorithm. For example, the selection of random state variables can be done in parallel by handling one variable per PE. Not all generated states will correspond to acceptable configurations, and hence, an accept/reject decision is necessary after evaluating the measure p (which involves global information from all processors). This part of the algorithm is similar to other simulation techniques such as simulated annealing.[68,131]

Another source of parallelism is in the computation of the function f for the value of the state variables generated above. In some cases, the evaluation of f may itself involve the solution of a very large system of equations. Hence, a large number of processors can be of great benefit. In some particle problems, the function f captures some thermodynamical quantity. The evaluation of the above integral relies on the ergodicity assumption that the average of f observed over a large series of system states will approach the integral value. In many cases, the probability distribution follows a Boltzmann law.

Finally, the secondary estimator is simply a summation over a range of primary estimators. If a large number of primary estimators is being pursued in parallel, some parallelism can be applied to this computation (see, for example, the solution of PDEs discussed in the next Section).

In many cases, the search for state configurations is dictated by a priori information, such as in physics modeling. For example, in **quantum-chromodynamics** (QCD) simulations, each processor generates a new state variable. This generation must conform to some local rules involving neighboring lattice points. A large number of PEs can be of significant value for QCD problems involving a large number of lattice points. The integrals addressed in the QCD simulations for the GF11 computer[19] involve over 2,000,000 variables.

A special purpose SIMD computer called GF11 has been created for solving QCD simulations.[19] The GF11 has a Benes-type network for communication.

11.11 Monte Carlo Solution of Patial Differential Equations

Solving partial differential equations by Monte Carlo methods is an interesting problem. In this section, a parallel algorithm will be shown for this problem. An interesting feature of the algorithm is that it requires unstructured communication at every communication phase. It is this feature that motivates the presentation of the technique in this section. From a PDE perspective, other approaches to solving partial differential equations may be more appealing.[180]

Suppose the following partial differential equation in two variables is given:

$$\frac{\partial F}{\partial t} = a \frac{\partial^2 F}{\partial x^2} + 2b \frac{\partial F}{\partial xy} + c \frac{\partial^2 F}{\partial y^2} + \cdots + f, \tag{3}$$

with boundary conditions $F(x, y, 0^+) = \phi(x, y)$, $(x, y) \in R$. A possible solving methodology consists of the following steps:

- Approximate the equation by finite differences on a grid in x–y plane.
- Solve the resulting linear equations by Monte Carlo.

This approach was used in the past and a computer for integrating these equations based on the above method has been proposed.[208]

The difference equation will be integrated at each node of the discrete grid in the plane. The key elements of the Monte Carlo method for the integration of the difference equation are as follows:

Primary Estimator: $Z(\psi)$ is based on random walks ψ starting at each node and terminating at an absorbing state. For example, the absorbing states are the boundary **R** of the region for elliptic equations. The specific form of this estimator depends on the particular coefficients of the difference equation. An example will be shown later in this section.

Transition Probabilities: $p[(x_i, y_j) ---> N_k]$, where N_k is a neighbor node of the current node (x_i, y_j). These probabilities are defined in terms of the coefficients of the PDE. The transition probabilities characterize the random walks through the grid nodes. Obviously, these numbers control the complete evolution of the integration method and can be chosen so that they define a probability measure. This is not possible for all second-order equations given by Eq. (3). For example, the hyperbolic case cannot be handled with this methodology.

Secondary Estimator: As usual, the secondary estimator is an average function of the primary estimations. Specifically,

$$F'(x_i, y_j) = \frac{1}{M} \sum_{i=1}^{M} Z(\psi_i)$$

converges in probability to the solution of the difference equation at (x_i, y_j) as M tends to infinity.[208]

In the following paragraphs, an example will be considered. Suppose the following Poisson equation, i.e., a particular case of the general elliptic problem, is given

$$\frac{\partial^2 F}{\partial^2 x} + \frac{\partial^2 F}{\partial^2 y} = f,$$

with $F(x, y) = \phi(x, y)$ on the border **R**. In this case, the estimators at each grid node P have the following form:

Primary estimator: $Z(\psi) = \phi(Q) - h^2 \sum_j f(P_j)$ at $P = P_0$, where h is the grid sampling distance.

Secondary estimator at P: $(1/M)\sum_{\psi(P)} Z(\psi)$.

In this special case, the transition probabilities are constant and identical in the north, south, east, west directions.

There are two phases in the implementation of a parallel algorithm for the above Monte Carlo technique. These are the setup phase and the running phase. These phases are characterized by the following steps:

- *Setup Phase:*
  1. Assign a PE per node (x_i, y_j) of the grid by a fixed rule (for example, row-major order if the region is a rectangle of nodes). Although the specific rule is not relevant, the chosen criterion should be known to all the PEs for the running phase of the algorithm. If there are not enough PEs, use the methods of Section 10.1 to simulate virtual processors.
  2. Each PE evaluates all PDE coefficients at its node (x_i, y_j) and determines transition probabilities from this node to all its neighbors. This information is kept in the PE as a short record consisting of coefficients and transition probabilities at (x_i, y_j).
  3. Mark all records (PEs) holding a boundary node. This marking is necessary to detect the completion of a random walk.

In the above sequence of operations, it has been assumed that the computation of the coefficients of the PDE at each grid node is an expensive process, and hence, it is done only once at the beginning of the algorithm. These values as well as the transition probabilities will be used many times in the running phase of the algorithm.

In the running phase, the algorithm proceeds so that each PE will integrate the finite difference, using the above Monte Carlo method, at a different grid node P. The way PEs are assigned to nodes in this integration process is almost immaterial, and the locality of the grid structure does not need to be preserved. It is essential, however, that each PE knows the address of the PEs that hold records computed in the setup phase.

On the other hand, if there are more PEs than grid points, then several processors can follow random walks starting at the *same* node contributing with several primary estimators for the same grid node. These PEs will, thus, cooperatively compute the secondary estimator. A word of caution is necessary here since the estimators shown above may be biased if termination rules for the random walk are imposed arbitrarily on the problem.

The specific steps of the running phase follow:

- *Running Phase:*
  1. All PEs generate one random neighbor P_{j+1} of the previously visited nodes P_j, according to transition probabilities computed in the setup phase.

2. Random access read: All PEs request relevant data about the new nodes P_{j+1} in parallel. These data were stored in a record in a certain PE determined by step 1 of the setup phase.
3. All PEs update their primary estimator. The computation depends on whether the visited node P_{j+1} is a boundary point or not.
4. If P_{j+1} is a boundary point, the corresponding PE concludes the current random walk. These processors have to update their secondary estimator, reset the current node to their corresponding starting point, and reset to zero the primary estimator.

As is clearly seen, the second step of the running phase involves unstructured communication among all participating processors. The reason is that after a number of iterations, each processor integrating the difference equations needs coefficient values and transition probabilities from a node whose location on the grid is completely random. All PEs issue a parallel read to fetch the data corresponding to the node they are visiting. Also, when a random walk is terminated, the PE starts a new walk from the original grid point. This means that some PEs will produce more primary estimations for some grid points. Termination rules for the complete algorithm must bear in mind that a fixed-time allocation for all the PEs may cut those random walks that are long, and hence, it may produce biased estimators. A statistical study of these effects is well beyond the scope of this paper, and the reader is referred to Ref. 103 for related information.

CHAPTER 12

Conclusions

In the previous chapters, a large number of parallel machines and algorithms have been examined. Although there are exceptions, many of the algorithms studied can be placed into one of three categories. The first category consists of algorithms that communicate only between processors that are adjacent in a two-dimensional mesh. These algorithms will be called mesh-type algorithms. Of course, all plain mesh connected computer algorithms are mesh-type algorithms, but many algorithms for pyramid computers and hypercube computers with weak independent communication are in this class. As shown in Section 10.2, hypercube-derived computers can also implement mesh-type algorithms efficiently in an asymptotic sense, but these implementations do not appear to be practical. No technique is known for implementing mesh-type algorithms efficiently on a plain hypercube.

Mesh-type algorithms are obviously well-suited to problems, such as $M \times M$ convolutions, that perform only local communication with a two-dimensional array. More surprisingly, these algorithms are also very efficient for some problems that require global communication. As long as the amount of computation that must be performed by each processor is at least proportional to $N^{1/2}$, there is the possibility of hiding the costs of the long distance communication. This is exactly the case for the Hough transform (assuming the number of projections, Q, is at least proportional $N^{1/2}$) and dense matrix multiplication. Finally, when the amount of computation required per processor is asymptotically less than $N^{1/2}$, the costs of global communication in a mesh-type algorithm cannot be hidden (in an asymptotic sense) by the cost of processing. However, there are some situations in which the constant of proportionality is quite small for the mesh-type algorithm, so even though the asymptotic performance is suboptimal, the algorithm could be very practical. Examples of such practical, though asymptotically suboptimal, mesh-type algorithms include the component shrinking algorithm and the log component shrinking algorithms given in Section 5.9 and the RAW and RAR algorithms for mesh connected computers with $O(N^{1/2})$ words of memory per PE given in Section 5.8.

The algorithms in the second category have communication that forms a binary tree, so they will be called tree-type algorithms. Tree-type algorithms run efficiently on pyramid, plain hypercube, and hypercube-derived computers. The fact that they cannot be implemented efficiently on plain mesh connected computers is a serious limitation of that architecture, and it is the reason that architectures that have both mesh and tree connections have also been considered. The most important set of tree-type algorithms consists of data independent parallel prefix operations. These include scans, segmented scans, broadcasting, determination of a maximum, and ranking.

The third category of algorithms consists of the class ascend and descend algorithms, and generalizations of those classes such as the bit-block algorithms. Such algorithms will be called cube-type algorithms. Cube-type algorithms run efficiently on plain hypercube and hypercube-derived computers. Although they cannot be implemented as efficiently on mesh connected computers, they still are often asymptotically optimal for such topologies. One example of such a cube-type algorithm is the bitonic sort. Cube-type algorithms are well-suited to problems which move large amounts of data long distances, such as sorting, permuting (static and dynamic, monotonic and arbitrary), pointer operations (RAW and RAR) and sparse matrix multiplication.

From the above considerations, the hypercube with weak independent communication appears to be the most useful of the computers that have been examined. Such a machine is able to implement mesh-type, tree-type, and cube-type algorithms very efficiently. If only mesh-type and tree-type problems need to be solved, the mesh connected computer with a tree is probably the best choice. The pyramid computer can also solve these two types of problems efficiently, but the added connections of the pyramid do not seem to help very much. If only tree-type and cube-type problems need to be solved, the hypercube-derived computers are satisfactory. The plain hypercube computer could also be used for these problems, but unless multiple dimensions can be used simultaneously, much of the communication hardware is not being used at any given time.

One somewhat surprising result is the practicality of mesh connected computers for a wide range of problems. It has been shown that they give optimal asymptotic performance for a wide range of problems, including some that require global communication. If a mesh connected computer is to be used for fast pointer-based communication, it seems best to have $P^{1/2}$ words of memory per PE and independent addressing. In fact, the existence of independent addressing is useful in all of the topologies. For example, table lookup operations clearly benefit from independent addressing.

So far the focus has been on the performance of different interconnection networks, but not on their costs. One of the most important factors in terms of cost is the number of wires required to leave each unit of packaging (e.g., a chip, board, or rack). One measure of the packaging costs can be obtained by examining the degree of the network. This corresponds to a level of packaging that has exactly one processor per unit of packaging. Another measure of packaging costs is given by the minimum bisection bandwidth (see Section 7.3). This corresponds to a level of packaging that has exactly one-half of the processors in each unit of ackaging.

Of course, many packaging issues lie between the extremes of one processor per unit and $P/2$ processors per unit. Formal models of the costs for such intermediate levels of packaging have been developed and analyzed by Snir[229] and by Cypher.[53] These models give costs for many different interconnection networks over a wide range of packaging levels. One result of these studies is that the hypercube can be surprisingly more expensive to package than the hypercube-derived computers. For example, consider a level of packaging for which each unit can hold $P^{1/2}$ processors. It has been proven that the number of wires leaving each unit of packaging in a hypercube is proportional to $\log^2 P$ times the number of wires leaving each unit of packaging in a hypercube-derived computer. It is surprising that the costs differ so widely, given that difference in the degrees is only proportional to $\log P$. The mesh connected computer requires significantly fewer wires leaving each unit of packaging than are required by either the hypercube or the hypercube-derived computers, thus partially compensating for its poorer performance on some problems.

Another issue in packaging is regularity. It is not practical to design a large number of different chips or boards for a single parallel computer. The mesh and hypercube are very regular and are easily decomposed into identical pieces. The hypercube-derived computers are more problematic, but as long as the sizes of the packaging are convenient, the leveled networks (the cube-connected cycles and butterfly networks) can be decomposed into identical pieces. The shuffle-exchange and de Bruijn topologies are irregular (they even have nodes with different degrees) and are very difficult to partition into a few different types of components.

Another challenge in parallel architecture is fault tolerance. Many of the algorithms that have been shown are carefully tailored to match a given topology. However, faulty processors or communication links could destroy this match between the algorithm and the topology. A few results demonstrating the ability to implement algorithms designed for a healthy topology on a faulty version of that topology have been obtained. For example, it has been shown that hypercubes[35,100] and hypercube-derived computers[12] maintain some ability to implement ascend and descend algorithms in the presence of faults.

Another very promising topology that has been suggested is the multibutterfly.[149,253] The multibutterfly is obtained by merging a number of different copies of butterfly networks that have been permuted in different ways. Upfal has shown that routing can be performed in $O(\log N)$ time on the multibutterfly, and Leighton and Maggs have shown that the multibutterfly is very fault-tolerant. As a result, the multibutterfly could be an important practical topology. Unfortunately, a fundamental property of the multibutterfly is its lack of locality, so it would presumably be difficult to package without having a large number of wires leaving each unit of packaging.

Bibliography

1. A. Aggarwal and M-D. A. Huang, "Network Complexity of Sorting and Graph Problems and Simulating CRCW PRAMS by Interconnection Networks," in *Proceedings of the 3rd Aegean Workshop on Computing*, 1988, pp. 339–350.
2. A. Aggarwal, "Optimal Bounds for Finding Maximum on Array Processors with k Global Buses," IEEE Trans. Computers Vol. 35, pp. 62–64, 1986.
3. N. Ahuja and S. Swamy, "Interleaved Pyramid Architectures for Bottom-Up Analysis," *International Conference on Pattern Recognition*, Munich 1982, pp. 388–390.
4. N. Ahuja and S. Swamy, "Multiprocessor Pyramid Architectures for Bottom-Up Analysis," IEEE Trans. Pattern Analysis and Machine Intelligence, Vol. 6, No. 4, pp. 463–475, 1985.
5. M. Ajtai, J. Komlos, and E. Szemeredi, "An $O(n \log n)$ Sorting Network," in *Proceedings of the 15th Annual Symposium on Theory of Computing*, 1983, pp. 1–9.
6. S. Akl, *Parallel Sorting Algorithms* (Academic Press, New York, 1985).
7. R. Aleliunas, "Randomized Parallel Communication," *ACM Principles of Distributed Computing*, pp. 60–72, 1982.
8. H. Alnuweiri and V. Prasanna Kumar, "Efficient Image Computations on VLSI Architectures with Reduced Hardware," *IEEE Workshop on Computer Architecture for Pattern Analysis and Machine Intelligence*, Seattle, WA, October 1987, pp. 192–201.
9. N. Alon, Y. Azar, and U. Vishkin, "Tight Complexity Bounds for Parallel Comparison Sorting," *27th Annual Symposium on Foundations of Computer Science*, October 1986, pp. 502–510.
10. R. Alverson, D. Callahan, D. Cummings, et al., "The Tera Computer System," in *Proceedings of the ACM Supercomputing*, 1990.
11. R. J. Anderson and G. L. Miller, "Deterministic Parallel List Ranking, in *Proceedings of the 3rd Aegean Workshop on Computing*, 1988, pp. 81–90.
12. F. Annexstein, "Fault Tolerance in Hypercube-derivative Networks," presented at the *1st ACM Symposium on Parallel Algorithms and Architectures*, June 1989, pp. 179–188.
13. R. Arlauskas, iPSC2 System: "A Second Generation Hypercube," in *Proceedings of the Third Conference on Hypercube Concurrent Computers and Applications*, 1988, pp. 38–42.

14. D. Auerbach, W. Paul, A. Bakker, et al., "A Special Purpose Parallel Computer for Molecular Dynamics: Motivation, Design, Implementation, and Application," Technical Report RJ 5431, Department of Physics, IBM Almaden Research Center, December 1986.

15. Y. Azar, U. Vishkin, "Tight Comparison Bounds on the Complexity of Parallel Sorting," Siam J. Computing, Vol. 16, No. 3, pp. 458–464, June 1987.

16. K. E. Batcher, "Sorting Networks and their Applications," in *Proceedings of the 1968 AFIPS Conference*, pp. 307–314.

17. K. E. Batcher, "Design of a Massively Parallel Processor," IEEE Trans. Computers, Vol. c-29, No. 9, September 1980, pp. 836–840.
K. E. Batcher, "Bit-Serial Parallel Processing Systems," IEEE on Computers, Vol. c-31, no. 5, pp. 377–384, May 1982.

18. G. Baudet and D. Stevenson, "Optimal Sorting Algorithms for Parallel Computers," IEEE Trans. Computers, Vol. c-27, No. 1, pp. 84–87, January 1978.

19. J. Beetem, M. Denneau and D. Weingarten, "The GF11 Parallel Computer," in *Experimental Parallel Computing Architectures*, edited by J. J. Dongarra. (North-Holland, Amsterdam 1987), pp. 255–298.

20. V. E. Benes, "Optimal Rearrangeable Multistage Connecting Networks," Bell System Technical Journal, Vol. 43, pp. 1641–1656, 1964.

21. J-C. Bermond and C. Peyrat, "de Bruijn and Kautz Networks: A Competitor for the Hypercube?," in *Hypercube and Distributed Computers*, edited by F. Andre and J. P. Verjus (Elsevier Science Publishers B.V. North-Holland, Amsterdam 1989), pp. 279–293.

22. S. N. Bhatt, F. R. K. Chung, J-W. Hong, et al., "Optimal Simulations by Butterfly Networks," presented at the *20th ACM Symposium on Theory of Computing*, May 1988, pp. 192–204.

23. V. Bhavsar and J. Isaac, "Design and Analysis of Parallel Monte Carlo Algorithms," Siam J. Scientific and Statistical Computing, Vol. 8, No. 1, pp. 73–95, January 1987.

24. R. Bianchini and R. Bianchini, Jr., "Wireability of an Ultracomputer," Courant Mathematics and Computing Laboratory, New York University, DOE ER 03077-177, October 1982.

25. G. Bilardi and A. Nicolau, "Adaptive Bitonic Sorting: An Optimal Parallel Algorithm for Shared Memory Machines," Technical Report 86-769, Department of Computer Science, Cornell University, August 1986.

26. R. P. Blanford, "Dynamically Quantized Pyramids for Hough Vote Collection," *IEEE Workshop on Computer Architecture for Pattern Analysis and Machine Intelligence*, October 1987, pp. 145–152.

27. D. Bitton, D.J. DeWitt, D.K. Hsiao, and J. Menon, "A Taxonomy of Parallel Sorting," Computing Surveys, Vol. 16, No. 3, pp. 287–318, September 1984.

28. G. Blelloch, "Applications and Algorithms on The Connection Machine," MIT Artificial Intelligence Laboratory, February 1987.

29. G. Blelloch, "Scans as Primitive Parallel Operations," in *Proceedings of the International Conference on Parallel Processing*, St. Charles, IL, August 1987, pp. 355–362.

30. D. Blevins, E. Davis, R. Heaton and J. Reif, "BLITZEN: A Highly Integrated Massively Parallel Machine," J. Parallel and Distributed Computing, Vol. 8, pp. 150–160, 1990.

31. S. H. Bokhari, "MAX: An Algorithm for Finding Maximum in an Array Processor with a Global Bus," *1981 International Conference on Parallel Processing*, August 1981, pp. 302–303.

32. A. Borodin and J. E. Hopcroft, "Routing, Merging and Sorting on Parallel Models of Computation," in *Proceedings of the 14th Annual Symposium on Theory of Computing*, 1982, pp. 338–344.

33. A. Borodin and I. Munro, *The Computational Complexity of Algebraic and Numeric Problems* (American Elsevier, New York, 1975).

34. R. Brodersen, invited presentation on VLSI and signal processing at the 21st Asilomar Conference on Systems, Signals, and Computers. Asilomar, CA, November 1987.

35. J. Bruck, R. Cypher, and D. Soroker, "Running Algorithms Efficiently on Faulty Hypercubes," *2nd ACM Symposium on Parallel Algorithms and Architectures*, July 1990, pp. 37–44.

36. L. E. Cannon, "A Cellular Computer to Implement the Kalman Filter Algorithm," Ph.D. thesis, Montana State University, 1969.

37. V. Cantoni and S. Levialdi, *Pyramidal Systems for Computer Vision*, NATO Advanced Science Institutes Series, Vol. 25 (Springer-Verlag, 1986).

38. V. Cantoni, M. Ferretti, S. Levialdi, and F. Maloberti, "A Pyramid Project Using Integrated Technology" in *Integrated Technology for Parallel Image Processing* (Academic Press, London, 1985) pp. 121–132.

39. V. Cantoni and S. Levialdi, "Matching the Task to an Image Processing Architecture," Computer Vision, Graphics, and Image Processing, Vol. 22, pp. 301–309, 1983.

40. L. Carter and M. Wegman, "Universal Classes of Hash Functions," J, Comput. Syst. Sci., Vol. 18, No. 2, pp. 143–154, 1979.

41. C. Chu, "A Sine Transform Algorithm for the Hypercube," Technical Report 87-825, Dept. of Comp. Sci., Cornell University, Ithaca, NY, March 1987.

42. P. Close, The iPSC2 Node Architecture, in *Proceedings of the Third Conference on Hypercube Concurrent Computers and Applications*, pp. 43–50, 1988.

43. E. R. Cohn and R. W. Haddad, "Beta Operations: Efficient Implementation of a Primitive Parallel Operation," Technical Report STAN-CS-86-1129, Department of Computer Science, Stanford University, August 1986.

44. R. Cole, "Parallel Merge Sort," *27th Annual Symposium on Foundations of Computer Science*, October 1986, pp. 511–516.

45. R. Cole and U. Vishkin, "Deterministic Coin Tossing and Accelerating Cascades: Micro and Macro Techniques for Designing Parallel Algorithms," *ACM Proceedings of Annual Symposium on Theory of Computing*, Berkeley, CA, May 1986, pp. 206–219.

46. R. Cole and U. Vishkin, "Approximate and Exact Parallel Scheduling with Applications to List, Tree and Graph Problems," *27th Annual Symposium on Foundations of Computer Science*, October 1986, pp. 478–491.

47. O. Collins, S. Dolinar, R. McEliece, and F. Pollara, "A VLSI Decomposition of the deBruijn Graph," J. ACM, Vol. 39, No. 4, pp. 931–948, Oct. 1992.

48. R. Colwell, C. Hitchcock, E. D. Jensen, et al., "Computers, Complexity, and Controversy," IEEE Computer, pp. 8–19, September 1985.

49. L. Cordella, M. J. B. Duff, and S. Levialdi, "Thresholding: A Challenge for Parallel Processing," Computer Graphics and Image Processing, Vol. 6, pp. 207–220, 1977.

50. L. Cordella, M. J. B. Duff, and S. Levialdi, "An Analysis of Computational Cost in Image Processing: A Case Study," IEEE Trans. Computers, Vol. c-27, No. 10, pp. 904–910, 1978.

51. R. Cypher, "Efficient Communication in Massively Parallel Computers," Ph.D. thesis, University of Washington, 1989.

52. R. Cypher, "A Lower Bound on the Size of Shellsort Sorting Networks," Siam J. Comput. Vol. 22, No. 1, pp. 62–71, 1993.

53. R. Cypher, "Theoretical Aspects of VLSI Pin Limitations," in *Proceedings of the 6th MIT Conference on Advanced Research in VLSI* (MIT Press, Cambridge, MA, 1990), pp. 314–327.

54. R. Cypher and C. G. Plaxton, "Deterministic Sorting in Nearly Logarithmic Time on the Hypercube and Related Computers," in *Proceedings of the 22nd Annual Symposium on Theory of Computing*, 1990, pp. 193–203.

55. R. Cypher and C. G. Plaxton, "Techniques for Shared Key Sorting," Technical Report RJ 7347, Computer Science Dept., IBM Almaden Research Center, March 1990.

56. R. Cypher and J. L. C. Sanz, "Optimal Sorting on Feasible Parallel Computers," Technical Report RJ 5934, Computer Science Dept., IBM Almaden Research Center, November 1987.

57. R. Cypher and J. L. C. Sanz, "Cubesort: A Parallel Algorithm for Sorting N Data Items with S-Sorters," J. Algorithms, Vol. 13, pp. 211–234, 1992.

58. R. Cypher and J. L. C. Sanz, "Optimal Sorting on Reduced Architectures," in *Proceedings of the International Conference on Parallel Processing*, 1988, Vol. III, pp. 308–311.

59. R. Cypher, J. L. C. Sanz, and L. Snyder, "Hypercube and Shuffle-Exchange Algorithms for Image Component Labeling," J. Algorithms, Vol. 10, pp. 140–150, 1989.

60. R. Cypher, J. L. C. Sanz, and L. Snyder, "The Hough Transform has $O(N)$ Complexity on $N \times N$ Mesh Connected Computers," Siam J. Computers, Vol. 19, No. 5, pp. 805–820, 1990.

61. R. Cypher, J. L. C. Sanz, and L. Snyder, "Algorithms for Image Component Labeling on SIMD Mesh Connected Computers," IEEE Trans. Computers, Vol. 39, No. 2, pp. 276–281, 1990.

62. R. Cypher, J. L. Sanz, and L. Snyder, "An EREW PRAM Algorithm for Image Component Labeling," IEEE Trans. Pattern Analysis and Machine Intelligence, Vol. 11, No. 3, pp. 258–262, March 1989.

63. W. J. Dally and C. L. Seitz, "Deadlock-Free Message Routing in Multiprocessor Interconnection Networks," IEEE Trans. Computers, pp. 547–553, May 1987.

64. P. Danielsson and S. Levialdi, "Computer Architectures for Pictorial Information Systems," IEEE Computer, pp. 53–67, Nov. 1981.

65. F. Darema-Rogers, G. Pfister, and K. So, Memory Access Patterns of Parallel Scientific Programs, Tech. Report, RC 12086, Computer Science, IBM T. Watson Research Center, 1986.

66. F. Darema-Rogers, "Parallel Application Development for Shared Memory Systems," Tech. Report, RC 12229, Computer Science, IBM T. Watson Research Center, 1986.

67. F. Darema-Rogers, D. George, V. Norton, et al., "A Single Program Multiple-Data Computational Modle for EPEXFORTRAN," Tech. Report, RC 11552, Computer Science, IBM T. Watson Research Center, 1986.

68. F. Darema Rogers, S. Kirkpatrick, and V. Norton, "Parallel Algorithms for Chip Placement by Simulated Annealing," IBM J. Research and Development, Vol. 31, No. 3, pp. 391–402, May 1987.

69. E. Dekel, D. Nassimi, and S. Sahni, "Parallel Matrix and Graph Algorithms," SIAM J. Computing, Vol. 10, No. 4, pp. 657–675, Nov. 1981.

70. J. E. Devaney, "The MPP—A Totally Different Approach to Programming," IEEE Workshop on Computer Architecture for Pattern Analysis and Image Database Management, Nov. 1985, pp. 420–427.

71. V. Di Gesu, "An Overview on Pyramid Machines for Image Processing," International Conference on Advances in Pattern Recognition and Digital Techniques, Indian Statistical Institute, Calcutta, New Delhi, India, 1986.

72. M. J. Duff, "CLIP 4: A Large Scale Integrated Circuit Array Parallel Processor," *IEEE International Joint Conference on Pattern Recognition*, Nov. 1976, pp. 728–733.

73. M. J. B. Duff, "Real Applications on CLIP4" in *Integrated Technology for Parallel Image Processing* (Academic Press, London, 1985), pp. 153–165.

74. M. J. Duff, "Review of the CLIP Image Processing System," *National Computer Conference*, Anaheim, CA, 1978.

75. M. J. Duff, "Real Applications on CLIP4," in *Integrated Technology for Parallel Image Processing*, edited by S. Levialdi (Academic Press, New York, 1985).

76. C. R. Dyer, "Programming Techniques for Hierarchical Parallel Image Processors," in *Multicomputers and Image Processing Algorithms and Programs* (Academic Press, New York, 1982), pp. 409–420.

77. C. R. Dyer and A. Rosenfeld, "Parallel Image Processing by Memory-Augmented Cellular Automata," IEEE Trans. Pattern Analysis and Machine Intelligence, Vol. PAMI-3, No. 1, pp. 29–41, 1981.

78. Z. Fang and X. Li, "Parallel Algorithms for Image Template Matching on Hypercube SIMD Computers," IEEE Workshop on Computer Architecture for Pattern Analysis and Image Database Management, Nov. 1985, pp. 33–40.

79. Z. Fang, X. Li, and L. Ni, "Parallel Algorithms for 2-D Convolution," *1986 International Conference on Parallel Processing*, Aug. 1986, pp. 262–269.

80. F. E. Fich, "New Bounds for Parallel Prefix Circuits," in *Proceedings of the 15th Annual Symposium on Theory of Computing*, 1983, pp. 100–109.

81. A. L. Fisher and P. T. Highnam, "Real-Time Image Processing on Scan Line Array Processors," *IEEE Workshop on Computer Architecture for Pattern Analysis and Image Database Management*, Nov. 1985, pp. 484–489.

82. A. L. Fisher and P. T. Highnam, "Computing the Hough Transform on a Scan Line Array Processor," *IEEE Workshop on Computer Architecture for Pattern Analysis and Machine Intelligence*, Oct. 1987, pp. 83–87.

83. J. P. Fishburn and R. A. Finkel, "Quotient Networks," IEEE Trans. Computers, Vol. c-31, No. 4, pp. 288–295, April 1982.

84. M. Flynn, "Some Computer Organizations and Their Effectiveness," in *Tutorial on Parallel Processing*, edited by R. Kuhn, D. Padua, (IEEE Computer Society, Los Alamitos, CA 1981).

85. M. Flynn, "Very High Speed Computing Systems," in Proceedings of the IEEE, Vol. 54, pp. 1901–1909, 1966.

86. G. Fox, "The First Year of the Parallel Supercomputer," in *Proceedings of the Fourth Conference on Hypercubes, Concurrent Computers and Applications*, March 6–8, 1989, Vol. 1, pp. 1–37.

87. S. Fortune and J. Wyllie, "Parallelism in Random Access Machines," in *Proceedings of the 10th Symposium on Theory of Computing*, 1978, pp. 114–118.

88. T. J. Fountain, "Plans for the CLIP7 Chip" in *Integrated Technology for Parallel Image Processing* (Academic Press, London, 1985), pp. 199–214.

89. G. Fox, "Questions and Unexpected Answers in Concurrent Computation," in *Experimental Parallel Computing Architectures*, edited by J. J. Dongarra (North-Holland, Amsterdam 1987).

90. M. Franklin and S. Dhar, "Interconnection Networks: Physical Design and Performance Analysis," J. Parallel and Distributed Computing, Vol. 3, pp. 352–372, 1986.

91. K. A. Frenkel, "Evaluating Two Massively Parallel Machines," Communications of the ACM, Vol. 29, No. 8, pp. 752–758, 1986.

92. R. Davis and D. Thomas, "Systolic Array Chip Matches the Pace of High-Speed Processing," Electronic Design, October 31, 1984.

93. F. A. Gerritsen, "A Comparison of the CLIP4, DAP and MPP Processor-Array Implementations" in *Computing Structures for Image Processing* (Academic Press, London, 1983), pp. 15–30.

94. P. Gibbons, "The Asynchronous PRAM: A Semi-Synchronous Model for Shared Memory MIMD Machines," Technical Report TR-89-062, Intl. Computer Science Institute, Berkeley, CA, December 1989.

95. A. Gottlieb and C.P. Kruskal, "Complexity Results for Permuting Data and Other Computations on Parallel Processors," J. ACM, Vol. 31, No. 2, pp. 193–209, April 1984.

96. A. Gottlieb, "An Overview of the NYU Ultracomputer Project," in *Experimental Parallel Computing Architectures*, edited by J. J. Dongarra, (North-Holland, Amsterdam, 1987).

97. C. Guerra and S. Hambrusch, "Parallel Algorithms for Line Detection on a Mesh," *IEEE Workshop on Computer Architecture for Pattern Analysis and Machine Intelligence*, Seattle, Washington, October 1987, pp. 99–106.

98. J. Halton, "A Retrospective and Prospective Survey of the Monte Carlo Method," Siam Review, Vol. 12, No. 1, pp. 1–62, January 1970.

99. S. Hart, "A Note on the Edges of the n-cube," Discrete Math., Vol. 14, pp. 157–163, 1976.

100. J. Hastad, T. Leighton, and M. Newman, "Fast Computation Using Faulty Hypercubes," in *Proceedings of the 21st Annual Symposium on Theory of Computing*, 1989, pp. 251–284.

101. J. Hayes, T. Mudge, Q. Stout, et al, "A Microprocessor-Based Hypercube Supercomputer," IEEE Micro, pp. 6–17, October 1986.

102. P. Heildelberger, A. Norton, and J. Robinson, "Parallel Quicksort Using Fetch and Add," Technical Report, RC 12576, IBM T. Watson Research Center, March 1987.

103. P. Heidelberger, "Discrete Event Simulations and Parallel Processing: Statistical Properties," Technical Report, RC 12733, Computer Science Dept., IBM T. Watson Research Center, May 1987.

104. D. Heller, "A Survey of Parallel Algorithms in Numerical Linear Algebra," Siam Review, Vol. 20, No. 4, pp. 740–777, October 1978.

105. M. Herbordt, C. Weems, and J. Corbett, "Message-Passing Algorithms for a SIMD Torus with Coteries," in *Proceedings of the Second Annual ACM Symposium on Parallel Algorithms and Architectures*, July 2–6, 1990, pp. 11–20.

106. D. Hillis, *The Connection Machine* (MIT Press, Cambridge, 1985).

107. D. Hillis and G. Steele Jr., "Data Parallel Algorithms," Communications of the A.C.M., Vol. 29, No. 12, pp. 1170–1183, December 1986.

108. D. Hirschberg, "Fast Parallel Sorting Algorithms," Communications of the A.C.M., Vol. 21, No. 8, pp. 657–661, August 1978.

109. W. Hollingsworth, H. Sachs, and A. Smith, "The Fairchild CLIPPER: Instruction Set Architecture and Processor Implementation," Report No. UCB/CSD 87/329, U. C. at Berkeley, January 1987.

110. R. Hockney and C. Jesshope, *Parallel Computers: Architecture, Programming, and Algorithms* (Adam Hilger, Bristol, England, 1983).

111. R. Hummel, "Connected Component Labelling in Image Processing with MIMD Architectures" in *Intermediate-Level Image Processing* (Academic Press, London, 1986), pp. 101–127.

112. Y. Hung and A. Rosenfeld, "Parallel Processing of Linear Quadtrees on a Mesh-Connected Computer," Tech. Report CAR-TR-278, Ctr. for Automation Research, U. of Maryland, College Park, MD, March 1987.

113. K. Hwang and F. Briggs, *Computer Architectures and Parallel Processing* (McGraw Hill, New York, 1984).

114. H. A. H. Ibrahim, J. R. Kender, and D. E. Shaw, "The Analysis and Performance of Two Middle-Level Vision Tasks on a Fine-Grained SIMD Tree Machine," IEEE Conference on Computer Vision and Pattern Recognition, June 1985, pp. 248–256.

115. Inmos Corporation, "IMS T800 Transputer, Inmos Corporation, Bristol, UK, 1986.

116. J. Ja'Ja', K. W. Ryu, "Efficient Techniques for Routing and for Solving Graph Problems on the Hypercube," Technical Report CS-TR-2216, Dept. of Computer Science, U. of Maryland, March 1989.

117. L. Jamieson, D. Gannon, and R. Douglass, *The Characteristics of Parallel Algorithms*, Scientific Computation Series (MIT Press, Cambridge 1987).

118. L. Jamieson, P. Mueller, and H. Siegel, "FFT Algorithms for SIMD Parallel Processing Systems," J. Parallel and Distributed Computing, Vol. 3, pp. 48–71, 1986.

119. S. L. Johnsson, "Combining Parallel and Sequential Sorting on a Boolean n-Cube," in *Proceedings of the International Conference on Parallel Processing*, 1984, pp. 444–448.

120. S. L. Johnsson and C-T. Ho, "Optimum Broadcasting and Personalized Communication in Hypercubes," IEEE Trans. Computers, Vol. 38, No. 9, pp. 1249–1268, September 1989.

121. H. Jordan, "Structuring Parallel Algorithms in an MIMD Shared Memory Environment," Parallel Computing, Vol. 3, pp. 93–110, 1986.

122. A. M. Jrad and R. W. Hall, "The OFC Enhanced Mesh Architecture: A Performance Study," *IEEE Workshop on Computer Architecture for Pattern Analysis and Machine Intelligence*, Oct. 1987, pp. 184–191.

123. C. Kaklamanis, D. Krizanc, and T. Tsantilas, "Tight Bounds for Oblivious Routing in the Hypercube," *2nd ACM Symposium on Parallel Algorithms and Architectures*, July 1990, pp. 31–36.

124. M. Kalos, "Monte Carlo Methods and the Computers of the Future," Ultracomputer Note #83, NYU, Courant Institute, April 1985.

125. A. Karlin and E. Upfal, "Parallel Hashing: An Efficient Implementation of Shared Memory," J. ACM, Vol. 35, No. 4, pp. 876–892, October 1988.

126. A. Karp, "Programming for Parallelism," Computer, Vol. 20, No. 5, pp. 43–57, May 1987.

127. E. W. Kent, M. O. Shneier and R. Lumia, "PIPE: Pipeline Image Processing Engine," J. Parallel and Distributed Computing, Vol. 2, pp. 50–78, 1985.

128. R. M. Karp and V. Ramachandran, "A Survey of Parallel Algorithms for Shared-Memory Machines," Technical Report UCB.CSD 88/408, U. of California at Berkeley, Computer Science Division, March 1988.

129. P. Kermani and L. Kleinrock, "Virtual Cut-Through: A New Computer Communication Switching Technique," Computer Networks, Vol. 3, pp. 267–286, 1979.

130. D. Kim and K. Hwang, "Mesh-Connected Array Processors with Bypass Capability for Signal. Image Processing," *Hawaii International Conference on System Sciences,* Jan. 1988.

131. S. Kirkpatrick, C. Gelatt and M. Vecchi, "Optimization by Simulated Annealing," Science, Vol. 220, No. 4598, pp. 671–680, May 1983.

132. D. E. Knuth, "The Art of Computer Programming," Vol. 3 of *Sorting and Searching* (Addison-Wesley, Reading, MA, 1973).

133. R. Koch, T. Leighton, B. Maggs, et al., "Work-Preserving Emulations of Fixed-Connection Networks," in *Proceedings of the 21st Annual Symposium on Theory of Computing,* 1989, pp. 227–240.

134. S. Konstantinidou and L. Snyder, "The Chaos Router: A Practical Application of Randomization in Network Routing," *2nd ACM Symposium on Parallel Algorithms and Architectures,* July 1990, pp. 21–30.

135. C. Kruskal, T. Madej, and L. Rudolph, "Parallel Prefix on Fully Connected Direct Connection Machines," in *Proceedings of the International Conference on Parallel Processing,* pp. 278–284, 1986.

136. C. Kruskal, L. Rudolph and M. Snir, "The Power of Parallel Prefix," IEEE Trans. Computers, Vol. C-34, No. 10, pp. 965–968, Oct. 1985.

137. D. Kuck, E. Davidson, D. Lawrie, and A. Sameh, "Parallel Supercomputing Today and the Cedar Approach," in *Experimental Parallel Computing Architectures,* edited by J. J. Dongarra (North-Holland, Amsterdam 1987).

138. M. Kumar and D. S. Hirschberg, "An Efficient Implementation of Batcher's Odd-Even Merge Algorithm and Its Application in Parallel Sorting Schemes," IEEE Trans. Computers, Vol. c-32, No. 3, March 1983, pp. 254–264.

139. H. T. Kung, "Why Systolic Architectures?," Computer, Vol. 15, No. 1, pp. 37–46, January 1982.

140. H. T. Kung, "Synchronized and Asynchronous Parallel Algorithms for Multiprocessors," in *Tutorial on Parallel Processing,* edited by R. Kuhn and D. Padua (IEEE Computer Society, 1981).

141. T. Kushner, A. Y. Wu and A. Rosenfeld, "Image Processing on MPP: 1," Pattern Recognition, Vol. 15, No. 3, 1982, pp. 121–130.

142. R. E. Ladner and M. J. Fischer, "Parallel Prefix Computation," J. A.C.M., Vol. 27, No. 4, pp. 831–838, 1980.

143. C. Lang Jr., "The Extension of Object-Oriented Languages to a Homogeneous, Concurrent Architecture," Technical Report 5014, Department of Computer Science, California Institute of Technology, May 1982.

144. H. Lang, M. Schimmler, H. Schmeck, and H. Schroder, "Systolic Sorting on a Mesh-Connected Network," IEEE Trans. Computers, Vol. c-34, No. 7, pp. 652–658, July 1985.

145. D. Lawrie, "Access and Alignment of Data in an Array Processor," IEEE Trans. Computers, Vol. c-24, No. 12, pp. 1145–1155, December 1975.

146. S.-Y. Lee and J. K. Aggarwal, "Parallel 2-D Convolution on a Mesh-Connected Array Processor," *IEEE Conference on Computer Vision and Pattern Recognition*, June 1986, pp. 305–310.

147. T. Leighton, "Tight Bounds on the Complexity of Parallel Sorting," IEEE Trans. Computers, Vol. c-34, No. 4, pp. 344–354, April 1985.

148. T. Leighton, personal communication, 1988.

149. T. Leighton and B. Maggs, "Expanders Might Be Practical: Fast Algorithms for Routing Around Faults in Multibutterflies," *30th Annual Symposium on Foundations of Computer Science*, October 1989, pp. 384–389.

150. T. Leighton, F. Makedon, and I. Tollis, "A $2n - 2$ Step Algorithm for Routing in an $n \times n$ Array with Constant Size Queues," in *Proceedings of the ACM Symposium on Parallel Algorithms and Architectures*, pp. 328–335, 1989.

151. C. Leiserson, Z. Abuhamdeh, D. Douglas, et al., "The Network Architecture of the Connection Machine CM-5," in *Proceedings of the ACM Symposium on Parallel Algorithms and Architectures*, pp. 272–285, 1992.

152. S. Levialdi, "On Shrinking Binary Picture Patterns," Communications of the ACM, Vol. 15, No. 1, pp. 7–10, 1972.

153. H. Li and M. Maresca, "Polymorphic-Torus: A New Architecture for Vision Computation," IEEE Workshop on Computer Architecture for Pattern Analysis and Machine Intelligence, Oct. 1987, pp. 176–183.

154. H. Li and M. Maresca, "Polymorphic-Torus Network," in *Proceedings of the International Conference on Parallel Processing*, August 1987, pp. 411–414.

155. B. Lint and T. Agerwala, "Communication Issues in the Design and Analysis of Parallel Algorithms," IEEE Trans. Software Engineering, Vol. SE-7, No. 2, pp. 174–188, March 1981.

156. J. Little, G. Blelloch, and T. Cass, "How to Program The Connection Machine for Computer Vision, "*IEEE Workshop on Computer Architecture for Pattern Analysis and Machine Intelligence*, Seattle, Wa., October 1987, pp. 11–18.

157. B. D. Lubachevsky, "Simple, Efficient Asynchronous Parallel Prefix Algorithms," in *Proceedings International of the Conference on Parallel Processing*, 1987, pp. 66–69.

158. Y. Ma, S. Sen, and I. Scherson, "The Distance Bound for Sorting on Mesh-Connected Processor Arrays is Tight," in *Proceedings of the 27th IEEE Symposium on Foundations of Computer Science*, 1986, pp. 255–263.

159. MasPar Computer Corporation, "MP-1 Family Data-Parallel Computers, MasPar Computer Corporation, 749 North Mary Ave., Sunnyvale, CA, 1990.

160. A. Merigot, B. Zavidovique, and F. Devos, "SPHINX, A Pyramidal Approach to Parallel Image Processing," *IEEE Workshop on Computer Architecture for Pattern Analysis and Image Database Management*, Nov. 1985, pp. 107–111.

161. R. Miller and Q. Stout, "Varying Diameter and Problem Size in Mesh-Connected Computers," in *Proceedings of the International Conference on Parallel Processing*, August 1985, pp. 697–699.

162. R. Miller and Q. Stout, "Data Movement Techniques for a Pyramid Computer," Siam J. Computing, Vol. 16, No. 1, pp. 38–60, February 1987.

163. T. N. Mudge, "Vision Algorithms for Hypercube Machines," *IEEE Workshop on Computer Architecture for Pattern Analysis and Image Database Management*, Nov. 1985, pp. 225–230.

164. D. Myers and G. Adams III, "Benchmarking and Performance Analysis of the CM-2," RIACS Technical Report 88.19, Research Institute for Advanced Computer Science, NASA Ames Research Center, Dec. 1988.

165. G. Nash, D. Shu, and C. Weems, "Hierarchical Heterogenous Architecture for Image Understanding," in *Advances in Machine Vision*, edited by J. L. C. Sanz, (Springer-Verlag, New York, 1988).

166. D. Nassimi and S. Sahni, "Data Broadcasting in SIMD Computers," IEEE Trans. Computers, Vol. c-30, No. 2, pp. 101–107, February 1981.

167. D. Nassimi and S. Sahni, "An Optimal Routing Algorithm for Mesh-Connected Parallel Computers," J. A.C.M., Vol. 27, No. 1, pp. 6–29, January 1980.

168. D. Nassimi and S. Sahni, "Bitonic Sort on a Mesh-Connected Parallel Computer," IEEE Trans. Computers, Vol. c-27, No. 1, pp. 2–7, January 1979.

169. D. Nassimi and S. Sahni, "Finding Connected Components and Connected Ones on a Mesh-Connected Parallel Computer," Siam J. Computing, Vol. 9, No. 4, November 1980.

170. D. Nassimi and S. Sahni, "Parallel Permutation and Sorting Algorithms and a New Generalized Connection Network," J. ACM, Vol. 29, No. 3, pp. 642–667, July 1982.

171. D. Nassimi and S. Sahni, "Parallel Algorithms to Set Up the Benes Permutation Network," IEEE Trans. Computers, Vol. c-31, No. 2, pp. 148–154, February 1982.

172. NCR Microelectronics Division, "Product Description ncr45cg72, NCR Corporation, Dayton, OH, 1984.

173. NCUBE, "Product Report, Ncube Corporation, 1815 N.W. 169th Place, Suite 2030, Beaverton, OR, 1986.

174. P. Nelson and L. Snyder, "Programming Paradigms for Nonshared Memory Parallel Computers," in *The Characteristics of Parallel Algorithms*, edited by L. Jamieson, D. Gannon, and P. Douglass, (MIT Press, Cambridge 1987).

175. M. Noakes and W. J. Dally, "System Design of the J-Machine," in Proceedings of the 6th MIT Conference on Advanced Research in VLSI (MIT Press, Cambridge, MA, 1990), pp. 179–194.

176. A. Norton and A. Silberger, "Parallelization and Performance Analysis of the Cooley-Tukey FFT Algorithm for Shared-Memory Architectures," Tech. Report, Computer Science, RC 11885, IBM T. Watson Research Center, 1986.

177. G. R. Nudd, R. D. Etchells, and J. Grinberg, "Three-Dimensional VLSI Architecture for Image Understanding," J. Parallel and Distributed Computing, Vol. 2, pp. 1–29, 1985.

178. S. Nugent, "The iPSC/2 Direct-Connect Communications Technology," in *Proceedings of the Third Conference on Hypercube Concurrent Computers and Applications*, 1988, pp. 51–60.

179. S. E. Orcutt, "Computer Organization and Algorithms for Very-High Speed Computations," Ph.D. thesis, Stanford University, 1974.

180. J. Ortega and R. Voigt, *Solutions of Partial Differential Equations on Vector and Parallel Computers* (SIAM, Philadelphia, 1985).

181. D. Padua and M. Wolfe, "Advanced Compiler Optimizations for Supercomputers," Communications of the A.C.M., Vol. 29, No. 12, pp. 1184–1201, December 1986.

182. J. Palmer, The NCUBE Family of High-Performance Parallel Computer Systems, in *Proceedings of the Third Conference on Hypercube Concurrent Computers and Applications*, 1988, pp. 847–851.

183. M. Pease, "An Adaptation of the Fast Fourier Transform for Parallel Processing," J. A.C.M., Vol. 15, No. 2, pp. 252–264, April 1968.

184. N. Pippenger, "Parallel Communication with Limited Buffers," in *Proceedings of the 25th Annual Symposium on Foundations of Computer Science, 1984,* pp. 127–136.

185. G. Pfister, W. Brantley, D. George, et al., "An Introduction to the IBM Research Parallel Processor Prototype (RP3)," in *Experimental Parallel Computing Architectures,* edited by J. J. Dongarra, (North-Holland, Amsterdam, 1987).

186. G. Pfister and A. Norton, "Hot-Spot Contention and Combining in Multistage Interconnection Networks," IEEE Trans. Computers, pp. 943–948, October 1985.

187. C. G. Plaxton, "Load Balancing, Selection and Sorting on the Hypercube," *1st ACM Symposium on Parallel Algorithms and Architectures,* June 1989, pp. 64–73.

188. C. G. Plaxton, "Efficient Computation on Sparse Interconnection Networks," Ph.D. thesis, Stanford University, 1989.

189. J. L. Potter, "Image Processing on the Massively Parallel Processor," IEEE Computer, Jan. 1983, pp. 62–67.

190. J. L. Potter, "The Massively Parallel Processor," (MIT Press, Cambridge, MA, 1985).

191. V. K. Prasanna Kumar and M. M. Eshaghian, "Parallel Geometric Algorithms for Digitized Pictures on Mesh of Trees," *1986 International Conference on Parallel Processing,* Aug. 1986, pp. 270–273.

192. V. K. Prasanna Kumar and V. Krishnan, "Efficient Image Template Matching on Hypercube SIMD Arrays," *1987 International Conference on Parallel Processing,* Aug. 1987, pp. 765–771.

193. V. K. Prasanna Kumar and C. S. Raghavendra, "Array Processor with Multiple Broadcasting," J. Parallel and Distributed Computing, Vol. 4, pp. 173–190, 1987.

194. V. K. Prasanna Kumar and D. Reisis, "Parallel Image Processing on Enhanced Arrays," 1987 International Conference on Parallel Processing, Aug. 1987, pp. 909–912.

195. V. Pratt, "Shellsort and Sorting Networks," Ph.D. thesis, Stanford University, 1972.

196. F. Preparata and J. Vuillemin, "The Cube-Connected Cycles: A Versatile Network for Parallel Computation," Communications of the A.C.M., Vol. 24, No. 5, pp. 300–309, May 1981.

197. F. Preparata, "New Parallel Sorting Schemes," IEEE Trans. Computers, Vol. c-27, No. 7, pp. 669–673, July 1978.

198. M. Quinn, *Designing Efficient Algorithms for Parallel Computers,* McGraw-Hill Series in Supercomputing and Artificial Intelligence, 1987.

199. M. Quinn and P. Hatcher, "Compiling SIMD Programs for MIMD Architectures," in *Proceedings of the 1990 IEEE International Conference on Computer Languages,* pp. 291–296.

200. A. Ranade, S. Bhatt, and S. L. Johsson, "The Fluent Abstract Machine," in *Proceedings of the 5th MIT Conference on Advanced Research in VLSI,* March, 1988, pp. 71–94.

201. A. Ranade, "How to Emulate Shared Memory," in *Proceedings of the 28th IEEE Symposium on Foundations of Computer Science,* 1987, pp. 185–194.

202. A. P. Reeves, "On Efficient Global Information Extraction Methods for Parallel Processors," Computer Graphics and Image Processing, Vol. 14, pp. 159–169, 1980.

203. A. P. Reeves, "Parallel Computer Architectures for Image Processing," Computer Vision, Graphics, and Image Processing, Vol. 25, pp. 68–88, 1984.

204. J. H. Reif, and L. G. Valiant, "A Logarithmic Time Sort for Linear Size Networks, J. ACM, Vol. 34, No. 1, pp. 60–76, January 1987.

205. R. Rettberg and R. Thomas, "Contention is No Obstacle to Shared-Memory Multiprocessing," Communications of the A.C.M., Vol. 29, No. 12, pp. 1202–1213, December 1986.

206. A. Rosenfeld, "Parallel Image Processing Using Cellular Arrays," IEEE Computer, pp. 14–20, Jan. 1983.

207. P. Ruetz and R. Brodersen, "An Image Recognition Systems by Using Algorithmically Dedicated Integrated Circuits," Machine Vision and Applications, an International Journal, Vol. 1, No. 1 (Springer-Verlag, New York, March 1988).

208. E. Sadeh and M. Franklin, "Monte Carlo Solution of Partial Differential Equations by Special Purpose Digital Computer," IEEE Trans. Computers, Vol. C-23, No. 4, pp. 389–397, April 1974.

209. K. Sado and Y. Igarashi, "Fast Parallel Sorting on a Mesh-Connected Processor Array," Technical Report, Dept. of Computer Science, Gunma University, Kiryu, 376 Japan, 1985.

210. M. R. Samatham and D. K. Pradhan, "The De Bruijn Multiprocessor Network: A Versatile Parallel Processing and Sorting Network for VLSI," IEEE Trans. Computers, Vol. 38, No. 4, pp. 567–581, April 1989.

211. P. A. Sandon, "A Pyramid Implementation Using a Reconfigurable Array of Processors," IEEE Workshop on Computer Architecture for Pattern Analysis and Image Database Management, Nov. 1985, pp. 112–118.

212. J. L. C. Sanz, "Computing Image Texture Features in Parallel Computers," IEEE Proceedings, 1988.

213. J. L. C. Sanz and R. Cypher, "Data Reduction and Fast Routing: A Strategy for Efficient Algorithms for Message-Passing Parallel Computers," Algorithmica, Vol. 7, pp. 77–89, 1992.

214. J. L. C. Sanz, E. B. Hinkle, and A. K. Jain, Radon and Projection Transform-based Computer Vision, Springer Series in Information Sciences, Vol. 16, (Springer, New York, 1988).

215. I. Scherson and S. Sen, "Parallel Sorting in Two-Dimensional VLSI Models of Computation, IEEE Trans. Computers, Vol. 38, No. 2, pp. 238–249, February 1989.

216. I.D. Scherson, S. Sen, and A. Shamir, "Shear Sort: A True Two-Dimensional Sorting Technique for VLSI Networks," in Proceedings of the 1986 International Conference on Parallel Processing, pp. 903–908.

217. H. Schmeck, H. Schroder, and C. Starke, "Systolic s^2-Way Merge Sort is Optimal, IEEE Trans. Computers, Vol. 38, No. 7, pp. 1052–1056, July 1989.

218. C. P. Schnorr, and A. Shamir, "An Optimal Sorting Algorithm for Mesh Connected Computers," in Proceedings of the 18th Annual Symposium on Theory of Computing, 1986, pp. 255–263.

219. H. Schomberg, A Transputer-Based Shuffle-Shift Machine for Image Processing and Recognition, in Proceedings of the 10th International Conference on Pattern Recognition, 1990, Vol. 2, pp. 445–450.

220. E. J. Schwabe, "On the Computational Equivalence of Hypercube-Derived Networks," 2nd ACM Symposium on Parallel Algorithms and Architectures, July 1990, pp. 388–397.

221. J. Schwartz, "Ultracomputers, ACM Transactions on Programming Languages and Systems," Vol. 2, pp. 484–521, October 1980.

222. C. Seitz, "The Cosmic Cube," Communications of the ACM, Vol. 28, No. 1, pp. 22–33, 1985.

223. C. Sequin, "VLSI Design Strategies," Report No. UCB/CSD 87/323, Computer Science Division, U. C. at Berkeley, January 1987.

224. D. H. Shaefer, D. H. Wilcox, and G. C. Harris, "A Pyramid of MPP Processing Elements—Experience and Plans," *Hawaii International Conference on System Sciences*, 1985, pp. 178–184.

225. M. Sharma, J. H. Patel, and N. Ahuja, "NETRA: An Architecture for a Large Scale Multiprocessor Vision System," *IEEE Workshop on Computer Architecture for Pattern Analysis and Image Database Management*, Nov. 1985, pp. 311–319.

226. Y. Shiloach and U. Vishkin, "An $O(\log n)$ Parallel Connectivity Algorithm," J. Algorithms, Vol. 3, pp. 57–67, 1982.

227. H. J. Siegel, T. Schwederski, N. J. Davis IV, and J. T. Kuehn, "PASM: A Reconfigurable Parallel System for Image Processing," Computer Architecture News, Vol. 12, No. 4, pp. 7–19, 1984.

228. T. M. Silberberg, "The Hough Transform on the Geometric Arithmetic Parallel Processor," *IEEE Workshop on Computer Architecture for Pattern Analysis and Image Database Management*, Nov. 1985, pp. 387–393.

229. M. Snir, "I.O Limitations on Multi-Chip VLSI Systems," in *Proceedings of the 19th Allerton Conference on Communication, Control and Computing*, 1981, pp. 224–233.

230. L. Snyder, "Type Architectures, Shared Memory and the Corollary of Modest Potential," Annual Review of Computer Science, Vol. 1, 1986.

231. L. Snyder, "A Taxonomy of Synchronous Parallel Machines," *International Conference on Parallel Processing*, 1988, pp. 281–285, Vol. I.

232. H. Stone, "Parallel Processing with the Perfect Shuffle," IEEE Trans. Computers, Vol. c-20, No. 2, pp. 153–161, February 1971.

233. Q. F. Stout, "Sorting, Merging, Selecting, and Filtering on Tree and Pyramid Machines," *1983 International Conference on Parallel Processing*, Aug. 1983, pp. 214–221.

234. Q. F. Stout, "Meshes with Multiple Buses," *IEEE Symposium on Foundations of Computer Science*, Oct. 1986, pp. 264–273.

235. J. P. Strong, "The Fourier Transform on Mesh Connected Processing Arrays such as the Massively Parallel Processor," *IEEE Workshop on Computer Architecture for Pattern Analysis and Image Database Management*, Nov. 1985, pp. 190–196.

236. H. Sullivan, T. Bashkow, "A Large Scale Homogeneous Machine," in *Proceedings of the 4th Annual Symposium on Computer Architecture*, 1977, pp. 105–124.

237. M. H. Sunwoo, B. S. Baroody, and J. K. Aggarwal, "A Parallel Algorithm for Region Labeling," *IEEE Workshop on Computer Architecture for Pattern Analysis and Machine Intelligence*, Oct. 1987, pp. 27–36.

238. *Second International Conference on Supercomputing*, Vol. I, II, III. Santa Clara, California, May 1987.

239. S. L. Tanimoto, A. Klinger (Eds.), *Structured Computer Vision: Machine Perception Through Hierarchical Computation Structures*, (Academic Press, New York, 1980).

240. S. L. Tanimoto, "Programming Techniques for Hierarchical Parallel Image Processors," in *Multicomputers and Image Processing Algorithms and Programs* (Academic Press, New York, 1982), pp. 421–429.

241. S. L. Tanimoto, "A Pyramidal Approach to Parallel Processing," *ACM International Symposium on Computer Architecture*, June 1983, pp. 372–378.

242. S. L. Tanimoto, "Algorithms for Median Filtering of Images on a Pyramid Machine" in *Computing Structures for Image Processing* (Academic Press, London, 1983), pp. 123–141.

243. S. L. Tanimoto, "A Hierarchical Cellular Logic for Pyramid Computers," J. Parallel and Distributed Computing, Vol. 1, pp. 105–132, 1984.

244. S. L. Tanimoto, T. J. Ligocki, and R. Ling, "A Prototype Pyramid Machine for Hierarchical Cellular Logic" in *Parallel Hierarchical Computer Vision*, edited by L. Uhr (Academic Press, London, 1987).

245. R. E. Tarjan and U. Vishkin, "An Efficient Parallel Biconnectivity Algorithm," Siam J. Computing, Vol. 14, No. 4, pp. 862–874, Nov. 1985.

246. P. S. Tseng, K. Hwang, and V. K. Prasanna Kumar, "A VLSI-Based Multiprocessor Architecture for Implementing Parallel Algorithms," *International Conference on Parallel Processing*, Aug. 1985, pp. 657–664.

247. C. Thompson, "A Complexity Theory for VLSI," Ph.D. thesis, Carnegie Mellon University Computer Science Department, 1980.

248. C. Thompson and H. Kung, "Sorting on a Mesh Connected Parallel Computer," Communications of the A.C.M., Vol. 20, No. 4, pp. 263–271, April 1977.

249. P. S. Tseng, K. Hwang, and V. K. P. Kumar, "A VLSI-Based Multiprocessor Architecture for Implementing Parallel Algorithms," in *Proceedings of the 1985 International Conference on Parallel Processing*, pp. 657–664.

250. L. Uhr, "Parallel, Hierarchical Software. Hardware Pyramid Architectures," Tech. Report #646, Dept. of Comp. Sci., U. of Wisconsin, Madison, WI, June 1986.

251. J. Ullman, *Computational Aspects of VLSI* (Computer Science Press, 1984).

252. E. Upfal, "Efficient Schemes for Parallel Communication," J. ACM, Vol. 31, No. 3, pp. 507–517, July 1984.

253. E. Upfal, "An $O(\log N)$ Deterministic Packet Routing Scheme," in *Proceedings of the 21st Annual Symposium on Theory of Computing*, 1989, pp. 241–250.

254. E. Upfal and A. Wigderson, "How to Share Memory in a Distributed System," J. A.C.M., Vol. 34, No. 1, pp. 116–127, January 1987.

255. L. G. Valiant, "Parallelism in Comparison Problems," Siam J. of Computing, Vol. 4, No. 3, pp. 348–355, September 1975.

256. L. G. Valiant, "A Scheme for Fast Parallel Communication, Siam J. of Computing, Vol. 11, No. 2, pp. 350–361, May 1982.

257. L. Valiant and G. Brebner, "Universal Schemes for Parallel Communication," *13th ACM Symposium on Theory of Computing*, May 1981, pp. 263–277.

258. B. Wagar, "Hyperquicksort—A Fast Sorting Algorithm for Hypercubes," in *Proceedings of the Second Conference on Hypercubes Multiprocessors*, 1987.

259. R. Wagner and Y. Han, "Parallel Algorithms for Bucket Sorting and the Data Dependent Prefix Problem," in *Proceedings of the International Conference on Parallel Processing*, August 1986, pp. 924–929.

260. A. Waksman, "A Permutation Network," J. ACM, Vol. 15, No. 1, pp. 159–163, January 1968.

261. A. Wallqvist, B. Berne, and C. Pangali, "Exploiting Physical Parallelism Using Supercomputers: Two Examples from Chemical Physics," IEEE Computer, pp. 9–21, May 1987.

262. C. C. Weems, S. P. Levitan, A. R. Hanson, et al., "The Image Understanding Architecture," COINS Tech. Report 87-76, U. of Mass. at Amherst.

263. C. Weems, S. Levitan, A. Hanson et al., "The Image Understanding Architecture," COINS Tech. Report 87-76, Computer and Information Science, University of Massachusetts at Amherst, 1987.

264. W. Wilcke, R. Booth, D. Brown, et al, "Design and Application of an Experimental Multiprocessor," Tech. Report, RC 12604, Computer Science Dept., IBM T. Watson Research Center, 1987.

265. S. S. Wilson, "The PIXIE-5000—A Systolic Array Processor," *IEEE Workshop on Computer Architecture for Pattern Analysis and Image Database Management*, Nov. 1985, pp. 477–483.

266. C. Wong and R. Fiebrich, "Simulated Annealing-Based Circuit Placement Algorithm on the Connection Machine," *IEEE International Conference on Computer Design: VLSI in Computers and Processors*, October 1987, pp.78–82.

267. C. Wu, T. Feng, *Tutorial: Interconnection Networks for Parallel and Distributed Processing* (IEEE Computer Society Press, 1984).

268. J. Wyllie, "The Complexity of Parallel Computations," Technical Report 79-387, Department of Computer Science, Cornell University, 1979.

269. G. Zorpette, "Large Computers," IEEE Spectrum, January 1993.

Index